TOWARD A SOCIAL REPORT

Toward a Social Report

by

The U.S. Department of Health, Education, and Welfare
with an Introductory Commentary by Wilbur J. Cohen,
Secretary of Health, Education, and Welfare, 1968, and
Dean, School of Education, The University of Michigan

Ann Arbor Paperbacks
THE UNIVERSITY OF MICHIGAN PRESS

HN
56
A47
1970

First edition as an Ann Arbor Paperback 1970
Introductory Commentary copyright © by
The University of Michigan 1970
All rights reserved
ISBN 0–472–06171–2 (paperback edition)
0–472–09171–9 (clothbound edition)
Published in the United States of America by
The University of Michigan Press and simultaneously
in Don Mills, Canada, by Longmans Canada Limited
Manufactured in the United States of America

AN INTRODUCTORY COMMENTARY

The idea of a Social Report for the United States is not a new one.* In 1929, President Herbert Hoover commissioned the President's Committee on Social Trends. Its report, *Recent Social Trends in the United States,* was issued in two volumes in 1933. The mandate of the Committee was to analyze significant societal factors in order to provide a basis for policy in the second third of the twentieth century. For many years *Recent Social Trends* served as a stimulus to those who were interested in public reporting of social conditions. The appearance of the *President's Annual Economic Report* and the various reports of the United Nations during the late forties and early fifties on social issues served to emphasize the need for a periodic report on domestic social issues.

The *Report of the World Social Situation* published periodically since 1952 by the United Nations has been a major factor in the stimulation of a report on the domestic social situation. If the UN could develop such a report for the world, why couldn't we develop a similar one for the United States? This question was considered from time to time without any results.

The discussion of this issue during the forties and fifties always ended up with the question of the need for more statistics on social conditions. The tremendous development of economic statistics during the thirties and forties had provided a solid basis for economic analysis and economic reporting which eventually resulted in the establishment of the Council of Economic Advisors and the Economic Report. Where was the comparable development in statistics on social conditions?

---

*For a more complete description of the background of a social report see Daniel Bell's "The Idea of a Social Report" in the spring 1969 issue of *The Public Interest* (No. 15), pp. 72–84.

Some small steps to expand social indicators relating to health, education, and welfare were taken during the period 1959–1966 by the publication of *HEW Indicators* and *HEW Trends*. Although the statistical indicators were traditional, they served to provoke discussion in the Department of Health, Education and Welfare of the need for more basic and insightful measures of social well-being.

In 1965, the Russell Sage Foundation commissioned an independent study of social change and social indicators. The result of the work of this study was published in 1968 as *Indicators of Social Change: Concepts and Measurement*. This book, edited by Eleanor Bernert Sheldon and Wilbert E. Moore, contains the contributions of sixteen eminent social scientists and deals with a broad range of social issues.

During 1965 and 1966 discussions between Professor Bertram M. Gross, S. Douglas Cater, and the author eventually resulted in the inclusion in President Johnson's message to Congress on March 1, 1966, of a recommendation dealing with social indicators and a social report.

With the cooperation of John W. Gardner, the then Secretary of Health, Education and Welfare, and William Gorham, Assistant Secretary of HEW for Program Coordination, plans were laid for the development of social indicators and a Social Report. The result of these efforts is *Toward a Social Report* which I submitted to President Johnson on January 11, 1969. The many people who contributed to this effort are indicated in the acknowledgments and the accompanying membership of the Panel on Social Indicators.

The effort to produce a comprehensive report was cut short by the presidential transition of January 20, 1969. Alice Rivlin, who had the major responsibility for the preparation of the draft of the Report, worked diligently against great odds to produce an acceptable document. Mancur Olson prepared innumerable drafts some of which were cut or dropped because of the lack of time. Because of the time limitation, we debated whether or not to issue a report at all. We also questioned whether to include some subjects in the finished manuscript where the material seemed too incomplete. Finally, in the closing days of December 1968, we chose to select seven major topics and to limit our aspirations by calling the document

Toward what we had planned to achieve and utilizing the most up-to-date statistics available.

Irving Kristol in his review of the Report in *Fortune* (August 1, 1969, pp. 168–169), stated that this "slim paperback is nonetheless an important book worthy of attention," even though it received little publicity in the national press because of the close proximity between the release of the Report and the inauguration of President Nixon. He noted that as the title indicated, the document is not a Social Report but "a step toward one. The step leaves a long way to go." He further chided me for being "wildly optimistic" in the statement I made in the covering letter to the President that "a first social report could be developed within two years."

Daniel Bell, in commenting on *Toward a Social Report*, stated:

> The idea of a social report is one whose time has come. . . . No society in history has as yet made a coherent and unified effort to assess these factors that, for instance, help or hinder the individual citizen . . . live a full and healthy life equal to his biological potential, which defines the level of an adequate standard of living, and which suggests what a "decent" physical and social environment ought to include. The document *Toward A Social Report* is the first step in the effort to make that assessment.*

Format of A Social Report

Many of the problems and issues with which a Social Report must deal are difficult to quantify. Because of these difficulties, the specific indicators and modes of analysis must, at the onset, be considered experimental. They must remain so until we can be assured that we have found the indices which truly reflect the social state of the nation.

There are, however, separate but interrelated steps which must be followed in the development of a Social Report. There must be a continuing process of developing the indicators, analyzing the relevant factors, and establishing social goals. Once the appropriate social indicator has been developed, the

---
*See previous footnote.

data must be analyzed both in terms of the factors which explain why well-being of a societal factor is at its current level and in terms of the requirements for improving the conditions. This analysis should be one of the most important functions of a Social Report.

The final component of a Social Report and probably its greatest contribution is the recommendation of national goals and objectives. These specific goals could serve as the basis for discussion of social policy just as the recommendations of the President's Economic Report provides the groundwork for discussions of fiscal policy.

While considerable work has been done in developing separate indicators and analyzing the reasons for their being at a particular level, little attention has been paid to the establishment of national goals. Probably the broadest study of this type was undertaken by the President's Commission on National Goals. The Commission, appointed by President Eisenhower, issued its report in 1960 under the title *Goals For Americans*. A significant portion of this document dealt with domestic issues and social goals. But much more needs to be done if we are to keep pace with the problems and potential of our nation. A Social Report must include a broad range of societal indicators. Because of the changing nature of our society, these indicators too must be subject to change.

The following indicators and goals, which are expressed in measurable terms in Table I, represent specific indicators of social change. Some deal with areas of health, education, and welfare. Others deal with social trends, such as women coming into the labor force, and vacations and leisure time in our society.

Obviously, people assign different priorities to these and other items of public policy. The goals are designed as a point of departure—to help in opening up the dialogue and debate which must take place before social action is possible.

Selecting two of the above indicators, infant mortality and the number of people living below the poverty line*, it is

*For a general idea of the social goals to be included in a Social Report on the subject of poverty see Wilbur J. Cohen, "A Ten-Point Program to Abolish Poverty," *Social Security Bulletin,* December 1968, pp. 3–13.

TABLE I

Indicator	Present Experience	1976–79 Goal
1. Infant Mortality (per 1,000 live births)	22.1 (1967)	12
2. Maternal Mortality (per 100,000 live births)	28.9 (1967)	15
3. Family Planning Services (for Low-Income Women 15–44)	1 million (1968)	5 million
4. Deaths from Accidents (per 100,000 population)	55.1 (1967)	50
5. Number of Persons in State Mental Hospitals	426,000 (1967)	50,000
6. Expectancy of Healthy Life	68.2 years (1966)	70.2 years
7. Three- to five-years-olds in school or preschool	35.2% (1967)	95%
8. Persons 25 and older who graduate from high school	51.1% (1967)	65%
9. Persons 25 and older who graduate from college	10.1% (1967)	15%
10. Persons in Learning Force	100 million (1967)	150 million
11. Percent of Major Cities with public Community Colleges	66% (1968)	100%
12. Number of first-year students in Medical Schools	10,000 (1967)	18,000
13. Handicapped Persons Rehabilitated	208,000 (1968)	600,000
14. Average Weekly Hours of Work—Manufacturing	40.6 (1967)	37.5
15. Labor Force Participation Rate for Women Aged 35–64	48% (1967)	60%
16. Average Annual Paid Vacation—Manufacturing	2 weeks (1967)	4 weeks
17. Housing Units with Bathtub or Shower	85% (1960)	100%

18. Percent of Population Illiterate	2.4% (1960)	0
19. Voters as a Percentage of Voting Age Population	63% (1964)	80%
20. Private Philanthropy as a percent of GNP	1.9% (1967)	2.7%
21. Public and Private Expenditures for Health, Education and Welfare as a percent of GNP	19.8% (1968)	25%
22. Percent of Population in Poverty	12.8% (1968)	0
23. Income of Lowest Fifth of population	5.3% (1967)	10%
24. Persons who work during the year	88 million (1967)	110 million
25. Life Expectancy	70.2 years (1966)	72 years

possible in Table II to see the continuum of selecting an index, determining an appropriate mode of analysis, ascertaining relevant casual factors and finally developing recommended social goals.

The statistic of infant mortality, for example, serves as one indicator of societal health. This information must be broken down by geographic regions and by racial and ethnic patterns before it can be analyzed. From this base the factors needed to decrease the rate of infant mortality should be determined. These factors include, for example, improving prenatal care, expanding health insurance coverage, establishing more health facilities and increasing the number of trained medical personnel.

Once all the relevant facts are ascertained, it is then possible to develop a set of goals. In the case of infant mortality, goals could be established which would set the rate at 20 per 1000 live births in 1973, 17 per 1000 in 1975 and so on. These could be revised from time to time on the basis of actual experience.

There is no uniformity of opinion concerning the involvement of the state in the promulgation of social goals. Kristol,

TABLE II

TWO ILLUSTRATIONS OF VARIOUS ELEMENTS IN DEVELOPING A COMPREHENSIVE PROGRAM OF SOCIAL INDICATORS AND THEIR USE IN A SOCIAL REPORT.

The Social Indicator	Measurement of Change in Social Condition	Analysis Provided in the Social Report	Social Goals
1. Infant Mortality: 22 per 1000 live births	Reduction in rate nationally, State, locally, census tract, etc.	A. Prenatal Care B. Postnatal Care C. Health Insurance D. Neighborhood Health Centers E. Training Midwives F. Birth Control	20 per 1000—1973 17 per 1000—1975 15 per 1000—1977 12 per 1000—1979
2. Poverty: 25 million persons below the poverty line; 12.8% of population below the poverty line	Reduction in numbers and rate by race, age location, etc.	A. Pockets of Poverty B. Hard-core Problems C. Income Maintenance Programs D. Education and Training	20 million—1973 15 million—1975 10 million—1977 0 —1979

in a portion of the concluding comments of his review of *Toward a Social Report* stated:

> Any kind of Social Report would, in the eyes of many, entail a danger: it could involve government in making the kinds of judgments of value that, in our political order, are the prerogatives of the individual citizen or of the organizations of which he is a voluntary member. This danger is not imaginary. If—perhaps one should say when —we do have a Social Report, it will be necessary to subject it to rigorous and skeptical criticism.
>
> But, when all is said and done, the risks involved weigh less in the balance than the potential benefits . . . *

Dangers to individual or collective freedom are certainly possible wherever government action is taken. I fear, however, that Mr. Kristol has overstated the perils inherent in a Social Report and underestimated the political processes in this country. Just as the *Annual Economic Report* has not become the tool for total state economic planinng, I do not anticipate that the Social Report will become the vehicle for comprehensive social control. This is not its intention and I do not assume it will become its function.

Following on Kristol's admonition about the perils of the establishment of social goals, Michael Springer in the March 1970 issue of the *Annals* states that if a Social Report is extended to its "logical limits . . . society is only rational when there is complete consensus on national goals and when the knowledge about how to achieve these goals is relatively complete."*

Here again, there is a misinterpretation of the intent of a Social Report. As will be explained more fully in the section below, the purposes of the report are to inform the public, highlight issues and suggest courses of action. It is not, however, assumed that there must be uniformity of opinion throughout the country before public policy can be developed. Such will not be the case, nor has it ever

Fortune Magazine, August 1, 1969, p. 169.

* "Social Indicators, Reports and Accounts," *The Annals,* March 1970, pp. 11.

been the situation in the political history of the United States.

Why a Social Report?

We live in a rapidly changing era, an era where many of the premises and assumptions about the social order are no longer valid. Change produces uncertainty and uncertainty breeds fear. Change becomes less threatening, however, if we possess a firm grasp of where we have been, where we are, and where we are going. A Social Report which contains significant social indicators and scholarly analysis of our position past, present, and future could make an important contribution in reducing the fear and anxiety which many members of our society feel. It could also aid us in forging an intelligent policy of national growth and a balanced and coordinated program of economic and social development.

A Social Report is crucially important for those who are in decision-making positions in both the public and the private sectors. While there is a wide recognition of many of our social ills, the full dimensions of the problems are not clearly defined. We know, for example, that some people are the victims of discrimination, that adequate health care is not provided to the entire population, that a certain percentage of our school-age youth do not finish high school, and that a number of people are living below the poverty line. What we do not know with sufficient clarity is the total extent of some of the problems or their full implications.

A Social Report could bring many of these issues into sharper focus and provide the information and analysis needed to foster governmental action. For many years, for example, it was commonly assumed that most of the people were receiving adequate health care. The advent of Medicare and Medicaid, however, proved that the contention of adequate health care for all was false. Large segments of the population were not and are not receiving health services. Now, serious consideration is being given to the development of comprehensive health insurance which holds the potential for making medical services available to more people.

Was it necessary to pass two laws to prove that many people

were not receiving adequate health care? It is quite possible that a social report which clearly analyzed health services and medical needs could have placed the facts before the American public. The clear, uncontradictable facts could have accelerated the process of the provision of adequate health services to all.

Once the extent of the problems is known, the social indicators and the recommended social goals could serve as the basis for discussion for the establishment of national priorities. There will always be a scarcity of the resources needed to solve all the nation's ills. A clear statement of the social problems and the social goals could point the way for the differential emphasis of needs on a range of competing demands.

The establishment of national policies must be made with appreciation of the fact that many of the social problems America faces are interrelated. We cannot deal with the issue of poverty without a consideration of racial discrimination. We cannot solve the problems of poor health without analyzing the effects of pollution, malnutrition, and poor housing on these conditions. A social report which sets out to provide a macro-analysis of the social well-being of the nation could help in the establishment of the needed relationships.

A Social Report will provide the private sector with information which may be important for its own programs. The solutions to societal problems cannot be solely a governmental concern. The construction of new living units, for example, will be performed by private corporations. Health care, while partially financed by government, will continue to be provided by independent physicians. Job discrimination will end only through the actions taken by business and industry. By identifying specific problems and needs and by setting forth specific goals, a social report could provide the private sector with the necessary guidance.

Finally, the Social Report could also serve as a means of determining the effectiveness of the programs designed to solve social problems. If for example, a prenatal care program is initiated, we must know the effects of the efforts in reducing the infant mortality rate. If we work on dropout prevention, we should be able to assess the influence of this work on increasing the number of high school graduates. Government needs this information to shape and possibly reshape its programs. In addition, the American people have the right to know how successful the public and private sectors have been in the programs they support.

Current Activities for A Social Report

The legislation necessary to enact the development of a social report was first presented in 1967 by Senator Walter Mondale of Minnesota in the form of the "Full Opportunity and Social Accounting Act." The bill calls for the establishment of a Council of Social Advisors, the publication of an annual Social Report, and the creation of a Joint Congressional Committee on the Social Report. Support for this piece of legislation has been growing. In 1969, for example, Senator Mondale was joined by twenty other senators in cosponsoring the bill.

By following this pattern, the president could have timely advice and information on which he could base his actions. The hearings and the Report of the Joint Committee on the Social Report could highlight the important issues so that we could make important decisions more consciously, more quickly, and with a greater degree of participation throughout our society. In addition, the Social Report could be studied in our colleges and universities and by business and labor and by the public. There is presently a division of opinion as to whether the Social Report should be issued separately by a Council of Social Advisors or whether the Council of Economic Advisors should be expanded to include this function and issue an annual Economic and Social Report.

Some observers believe that the success of the Council of Economic Advisors is a strong reason for widening its functions. In addition, by creating a direct relationship of economic and social factors, both would be strengthened.

I believe, however, that they should remain separate, though a strong relationship should exist between the two. The types of data to be collected and analyzed are quite different in the two documents. Questions of employment or foreign trade are much more amenable to quantification than are the social indicators. Second, questions with which the Council of Economic Advisors deal are of a high enough inportance that they should be the sole focus of the Economic Council.

At any rate, it is imperative that we have a comprehensive Social Report as soon as possible. In the meantime, *Toward A Social Report* is intended to provide basic information, social indicators, and realistic goals on a selected number of important issues and thus to provide a sound basis for discussion of key social problems.

Commentary

America is currently facing the most complex and challenging issues it has confronted in the nearly 200 years of its existence as a Republic. Today there are deep divisions in our society:

— Between the young and the old
— Between the black and the white
— Between the rich and the poor
— Between students and their educational institutions
— Between those in our society who have power and those who feel powerless.

Out of these divisions have come the great social issues of the seventies, issues which are engaging the energies of public officials at all levels—federal, state, and local and in all branches of government, executive, legislative and judicial. In addition, these issues have involved the concerns of all our citizens. Some of the issues and some of the steps which could be taken are in the following areas:

Health and Illness

To improve the state of health and health care:

— That Medicare be extended to totally disabled people, no matter what their age. The disabled are faced with the same problems as the aged: heavy medical expenses at a time when their income and earning power are very low. Permanently and totally disabled social security beneficiaries can be included in the Medicare program on a sound basis.
— That the doctor-bill part of Medicare be put on the same social insurance prepayment basis as the hospital part.

— That at least part of the cost of prescription drugs, which can be unusually heavy for an older or disabled person, be covered under Medicare.
— That a reasonable cost range for all drugs should be used in all federal supported programs.
— That a Commission on Health Care Insurance, consisting of distinguished representatives of the consuming public, the health professions, and insurance carriers be appointed to recommend the precise form of comprehensive protection against the economic burdens of catastrophich illness. This would result in all persons being covered on an economical and efficient basis.
— That while this Commission is completing its study, most of the available private, as well as public, insurance coverage be broadened to provide coverage for a full range of preventive, ambulatory, and diagnostic care; and to cover such health problems as alcoholism or mental illness. If public and private third-party payers fully covered preventive and diagnostic services (like outpatient services), patients would make greater use of less costly health resources outside of hospitals and the long-run costs of Medicaid would be reduced.
— That hospital incentives to reward efficiency without compromising medical care be rapidly expanded. Once effective means of controlling hospital costs have been demonstrated, they could be extended in Medicare, Medicaid, and Maternal and Child Health Programs. Successful businesses must provide high-quality services at the lowest reasonable costs. We should help our hospitals do the same.
— That physicians and hospitals should voluntarily restrain prices increases in order to avoid restrictive controls.
— That comprehensive prenatal care be extended to all women of low-income families, so that, as far as possible, all children be born well.
— That family planning be included as a part of comprehensive health care to these women so that every child is born a wanted child. Family planning should no

longer be the quiet privilege of the well-to-do. It must be an integral part of our efforts to reduce poverty, raise educational levels, and so give people greater freedom of choice.

— That medical care for all children in low-income families be provided during the first year of life, placing special emphasis on nutrition, on the prevention or early correction of crippling disabilities, and on dental care. Once this program—which we call "Kiddicare"—is established, that it be stretched over a five-year period, so that the children covered would be assured of medical care until they reach the age of six.

— That financial incentives be offered to encourage the development of prepaid group practice groups, expanded community hospital outpatient services, and other plans offering promise of greater efficiency, more comprehensive service, and the like; and that the reimbursement policies of public and private insurers reflect the increased efficiencies of such providers.

— That overly restrictive State laws now impeding the use of new kinds of health manpower be substantially revised so that we can properly use the talents of technicians and aides in medicine, dentistry, nursing, and pharmacy.

Education

To help insure that all school-age youth receive the best possible education:

— That legislation be passed to provide Federal financial aid to school districts which have an approved plan of desegregation for school construction, teachers' salaries, and other needed services where such school districts demonstrate a fiscal incapacity to carry out such plans.

— That within the next four years today's Federal share of 8 percent of elementary and secondary school expenditures be sharply increased year by year, from $1.5 billion to the full authorization of $3.5 billion annually.

— That, to assure that all funds for education are well spent, we encourage and support the national assessment of

the state of learning in the United States, already authorized by Congress.
— That the property tax—the chief source of revenue for the schools—be modified, supplemented by other sources of revenue, and eventually eliminated.
— That Head Start be extended for low-income children, for all handicapped children, and ultimately for all children who could benefit, urban and rural—first for five-year-olds, then for four-year-olds, then for three-year-olds.
— That effective follow-up for preschool programs, incentives to attract highly qualified teachers to work with disadvantaged children, and use of advanced educational equipment and of individual tutoring be implemented.
— That new school construction and operating fund programs to improve the quality of education be started.
— That schools should serve as vital centers of community activity; that school systems should be developed which strengthen community ties with the schools and encourage real parental participation.
— That federal support to help school systems seeking to convert to full-year education be started with schools for disadvantaged children.
— That we triple the number and dramatically improve the quality of opportunities in vocational education under the new Vocational Education legislation.
— That we develop a whole series of continuing education programs—through vocational and technical schools, junior colleges and universities, educational television, community schools—and any other possible resource.
— That the expansion of Federal student-aid programs be undertaken.
— That cost-of-education allowances be paid to every institution which enrolls a federally aided student (undergraduate and graduate).
— That a variety of aids for graduate education and research to strengthen graduate research and increase the number of centers of excellence be expanded.

Welfare

To reduce the extent of poverty in America:

- That a greatly expanded program of work incentives, and opportunities for productive and self-supporting work be established.
- That the government establish a national Federal welfare payment, financed entirely by the Federal government and administered according to national standards, to be available to all individuals in need in the nation. Such a system would include financial incentives for men and women to seek employment, adequate day care for the children of working mothers, an effective job training program, legal protection, social services, and family planning services.
- That the social security program be broadened and increased to provided a basic minimum protection compatible with decency and health.
- That the appropriations and authorization for child welfare services (foster care, adoption, care of abused children) be increased, in order that all children and families in the nation will have a better chance to lead productive and meaningful lives.

Physical Environment

To increase the quality of our environment:

- That an expansion of our efforts to reduce air and water water pollution—two of the greatest threats to man's health and economy—take place.
- That application be made of all of our knowledge to reduce accidental deaths and injuries, and that occupational health programs be expanded.
- That the threat of food contamination which causes food-borne disease be eliminated.
- That we eliminate substandard and unsafe drinking water supplies.
- That we protect the American people from exposure to all harmful radiation.

— That an increase of our efforts to control community noise take place.
— That we expand and improve our methods of solid-waste management.
— That we increase our efforts to reduce home and neighborhood environmental health problems, including a drastic reduction of the number of rats in the United States.
— That we expand research and evaluation of the effects of environmental stresses on the individual.

If we are to grapple successfully with these issues and find solutions to the problems facing this nation, then it is essential that we have the best possible information and best possible analyses that can be available. A Social Report can be of untold assistance in this pursuit.

June 1970

WILBUR J. COHEN
Dean, School of Education
The University of Michigan

SELECT BIBLIOGRAPHY*

Bauer, Raymond A. (Ed.). *Social Indicators.* Cambridge, Mass.: M.I.T. Press, 1966.

Bell, Daniel. "The Idea of a Social Report." *The Public Interest,* No. 15 (Spring, 1969), 72–84.

Gross, Bertram (Ed.). "Social Goals and Indicators for American Society, Vol. I." *The Annals,* Vol. 371 (May 1967), 1–178.

Gross, Bertram (Ed.). "Social Goals and Indicators for American Society, Vol. II." *The Annals,* Vol. 373 (September 1967), 1–218.

Gross, Bertram and Michael Springer (Eds.). "Political Intelligence for America's Future," *The Annals,* Vol. 388 (March 1970), 1–132.

Gross, Bertram. *The State of the Nation.* London: Tavistock Publications, 1966.

Kristol, Irving. "Review of 'Toward a Social Report.'" *Fortune Magazine.* August 1, 1969, 168–169.

Olson, Mancur, Jr. "The Plan and Purpose of a Social Report." *The Public Interest,* No. 15 (Spring, 1967), p. 85–97.

Russett, Bruce M., et. al. *World Handbook of Political and Social Indicators.* New Haven: Yale University Press, 1964.

Sheldon, Eleanor B. and Wilbert E. Moore (Eds.). *Indicators of Social Change: Concepts and Measurement.* New York: Russell Sage Foundation, 1968.

United Nations: Department of Economic and Social Affairs. *Report on the World Social Situation.* New York: United Nations, since 1952.

U.S. Department of Health, Education and Welfare. *Annual Report 1968.* Washington, D.C.: Government Printing Office, 1969.

U.S. Department of Health, Education and Welfare. *Health and Welfare Indicators.* Washington, D.C.: Government Printing Office.

U.S. Department of Health, Education and Welfare. *Health, and Welfare Trends.* Washington, D.C.: Government Printing Office.

U.S. President's Commission on National Goals. *Goals for Americans.* Englewood Cliffs, N.J.: Prentice-Hall, Inc., 1960.

U.S. President's Research Committee on Social Trends. *Recent Social Trends in the United States* (2 vols.). New York: McGraw Hill Book Co., 1933.

U.S. President. *The Economic Report of the President.* Washington, D.C.: Government Printing Office, Annual since 1947.

U.S. Senate, Committee on Government Operations, Subcommittee on Government Research, 90th Congress., 1st Sess., Hearings on the Full Opportunity and Social Accounting Act (S. 843). Parts I, II, III, 1967.

*For a more complete bibliography, see Carol Agoc's "Social Indicators: Selected Readings," *The Annals,* vol. 388 (March, 1970), 129–132.

THE SECRETARY OF HEALTH, EDUCATION, AND WELFARE
WASHINGTON

January 11, 1969.

DEAR MR. PRESIDENT:

In March of 1966, you directed the Secretary of Health, Education and Welfare to search for ways to improve the Nation's ability to chart its social progress. In particular, you asked this Department "to develop the necessary social statistics and indicators to supplement those prepared by the Bureau of Labor Statistics and the Council of Economic Advisers. With these yardsticks, we can better measure the distance we have come and plan for the way ahead."

I have the honor to submit a report which reflects our efforts as of this time to assemble some relevant information that will lead to the development of such yardsticks. It deals with such aspects of the quality of American life as: health and illness; social mobility; the physical environment; income and poverty; public order and safety; learning, science, and art; and participation and alienation.

This document represents a preliminary step toward the evolution of a regular system of social reporting. We are offering it for the widest possible discussion, comment, and suggestion. We believe that it warrants the critical review not only of the Executive Branch and of the Congress, but also of State and local officials, the academic community, and leaders of business and industry.

I strongly recommend the continued allocation of staff resources in the Executive Branch to prepare a comprehensive social report to the Nation with emphasis on the development of social indicators which will measure social change and be useful in establishing social goals. With the preliminary steps already developed under your leadership I believe a first Social Report could be developed within two years. In our complex social order, it is difficult to measure the condition of any society. We need to examine additional areas of American life before we can arrive at a comprehensive social report. Moreover, we need to develop far more refined and varied techniques for measuring social conditions than are currently available. These additional steps should be taken promptly.

It is important to our Nation's future to examine the qualitative condition of society regularly and comprehensively. An accurate assessment of our social well-being is essential so that we can make informed decisions about priorities and directions in this Nation's social programs. It is our hope that "Toward a Social Report" paves the way for such an annual assessment.

Respectfully,

Wilbur J. Cohen

Secretary.

The PRESIDENT,
The White House,
Washington, D.C.

Acknowledgments

In 1966, John W. Gardner, then Secretary of Health, Education, and Welfare, invited a distinguished group of social scientists to advise the Department on the measurement of social change and the possible preparation of a Social Report. Their names are listed below. These social scientists, along with representatives of a number of Departments of the Government, were organized in the Panel on Social Indicators, which met several times for lively discussions of social reporting. Many Panel members also contributed materials which have been extremely useful in the preparation of the present report. Particularly heavy reliance has been placed on materials submitted by Otis Dudley Duncan, Myrick Freeman, and Harvey Perloff. Daniel Bell gave generously of his time and talents. The report itself, however, was prepared by the staff of the Department of Health, Education, and Welfare, and was not reviewed by the Panel. The Panel therefore bears no responsibility for the contents of this report.

The report was prepared in the Office of Alice M. Rivlin, Assistant Secretary for Planning and Evaluation, under the direction of Mancur Olson, Deputy Assistant Secretary for Social Indicators. Pamela Kacser, Martin Kramer, Isabel Sawhill, and Jane Breiseth made major contributions to the report; and Irving Goldberg and John Corson made many helpful editorial suggestions. Many others, both inside and outside the Government, provided important help and criticism. Miss Jacqueline Grover merits special acknowledgment for outstanding duty as editorial assistant.

PANEL ON SOCIAL INDICATORS

Daniel Bell—Cochairman
Columbia University

Alice M. Rivlin—Cochairman
Assistant Secretary
Department of Health, Education, and Welfare

Henry Aaron
University of Maryland

Raymond A. Bauer
Harvard Graduate School of Business Administration

Barbara Bergmann
University of Maryland

Albert Biderman
Bureau of Social Science Research

William G. Bowen
Princeton University

Oliver Bryk
Research Analysis Corporation

Ewan Clague
Department of Labor

James Coleman
Johns Hopkins University

Gerhard Colm
National Planning Association

Otis Dudley Duncan
University of Michigan

G. Franklin Edwards
Howard University

Solomon Fabricant
National Bureau of Economic Research

Martin Feldstein
Harvard University

Joseph Fisher
Resources for the Future, Inc.

Howard E. Freeman
Brandeis University

Myrick Freeman, III
Bowdoin College

Victor Fuchs
National Bureau of Economic Research

William Gorham[*]
Urban Institute

Bertram Gross
Wayne State University

Philip Hauser
University of Chicago

MADELYN KAFOGLIS
University of Florida

JOHN KAIN
Harvard University

CARL KAYSEN
The Institute for Advanced Study

FRANCIS KEPPEL
General Learning Corporation

SAMUEL LUBELL
Columbia University

ISADOR LUBIN
The Twentieth Century Fund

ROBERT MCGINNIS
Cornell University

CLARENCE MONDALE
George Washington University

DANIEL MOYNIHAN
Joint Center for Urban Studies of MIT and Harvard

SELMA MUSHKIN
State and Local Finances

HARVEY PERLOFF
Resources for the Future, Inc.

FREDERIC L. PRYOR
Swarthmore College

MELVIN REDER
Stanford University

STUART RICE
Surveys and Research Corporation

T. W. SCHULTZ
The University of Chicago

HARRY M. SCOBLE
*University of California
Los Angeles, California*

ELEANOR SHELDON
Russell Sage Foundation

NEIL SMELSER
*University of California
Berkeley, California*

ANNE SOMERS
Princeton, New Jersey

RALPH W. TYLER
Science Research Assoc., Inc.

MARVIN E. WOLFGANG
University of Pennsylvania

*Cochairman of Panel until May, 1968.

CONTENTS

	Page
LETTER OF TRANSMITTAL	iii
INTRODUCTION AND SUMMARY	xi

Chapter
I—HEALTH AND ILLNESS 1
Are we becoming healthier?

Chapter
II—SOCIAL MOBILITY 15
How much opportunity is there?

Chapter
III—OUR PHYSICAL ENVIRONMENT 27
Are conditions improving?

Chapter
IV—INCOME AND POVERTY 41
Are we better off?

Chapter
V—PUBLIC ORDER AND SAFETY 55
What is the impact of crime on our lives?

Chapter
VI—LEARNING, SCIENCE, AND ART 65
How much are they enriching society?

Chapter
VII—PARTICIPATION AND ALIENATION 79
What do we need to learn?

Appendix—*How can we do better social reporting in the future?* .. 95

INTRODUCTION AND SUMMARY

The Nation has no comprehensive set of statistics reflecting social progress or retrogression. There is no Government procedure for periodic stocktaking of the social health of the Nation. The Government makes no Social Report.

We do have an Economic Report, required by statute, in which the President and his Council of Economic Advisors report to the Nation on its economic health. We also have a comprehensive set of economic indicators widely thought to be sensitive and reliable. Statistics on the National Income and its component parts, on employment and unemployment, on retail and wholesale prices, and on the balance of payments are collected annually, quarterly, monthly, sometimes even weekly. These economic indicators are watched by Government officials and private citizens alike as closely as a surgeon watches a fever chart for indications of a change in the patient's condition.

Although nations got along without economic indicators for centuries, it is hard to imagine doing without them now. It is hard to imagine governments and businesses operating without answers to questions which seem as ordinary as: What is happening to retail prices? Is National Income rising? Is unemployment higher in Chicago than in Detroit? Is our balance of payments improving?

Indeed, economic indicators have become so much a part of our thinking that we have tended to equate a rising National Income with national well-being. Many are surprised to find unrest and discontent growing at a time when National Income is rising so rapidly. It seems paradoxical that the economic indicators are generally registering continued progress—rising income, low unemployment—while the streets and the newspapers are full of evidence of growing discontent—burning and looting in the ghetto, strife on the campus, crime in the street, alienation and defiance among the young.

Why have income and disaffection increased at the same time? One reason is that the recent improvement in standards of living, along with new social legislation, have generated new expectations—expectations that have risen faster than reality could improve. The result has been disappointment and disaffection among a sizeable number of Americans.

It is not misery, but advance, that fosters hope and raises expectations. It has been wisely said that the conservatism of the destitute is as profound as that of the privileged. If the Negro American did not protest as much in earlier periods of history as today, it was not for lack of cause, but for lack of hope. If in earlier periods of history we had few programs to help the poor, it was not for lack of poverty, but because society did not care and was not under pressure to help the poor. If the college students of the fifties did not protest as often as those of today, it was not for lack of evils to condemn, but probably because hope and idealism were weaker then.

The correlation between improvement and disaffection is not new. Alexis de Tocqueville observed such a relationship in eighteenth century France: "The evil which was suffered patiently as inevitable, seems unendurable as soon as the idea of escaping from it crosses men's minds. All the abuses then removed call attention to those that remain, and they now appear more galling. The evil, it is true, has become less, but sensibility to it has become more acute."

Another part of the explanation of the paradox of prosperity and rising discontent is clearly that "money isn't everything." Prosperity itself brings its own problems. Congestion, noise, and pollution are byproducts of economic growth which make the world less livable. The large organizations which are necessary to harness modern technology make the individual feel small and impotent. The concentration on production and profit necessary to economic growth breeds tension, venality, and neglect of "the finer things."

Why a Social Report or Set of Social Indicators?

Curiosity about our social condition would by itself justify an attempt to assess the social health of the Nation. Many people want answers to questions like these: Are we getting healthier? Is pollution increasing? Do children learn more than they used to? Do people have more satisfying jobs than they used to? Is crime increasing? How many people are really alienated? Is the American dream of rags to riches a reality? We are interested in the answers to such questions partly because they would tell us a good deal about our individual and social well-being. Just as we need to measure our incomes, so we need "social indicators," or measures of other dimensions of our welfare, to get an idea how well off we really are.

A social report with a set of social indicators could not only satisfy our curiosity about how well we are doing, but it could also improve public policymaking in at least two ways. First, it could give social problems more visibility and thus make possible more informed judgments about national priorities. Second, by providing insight into how different measures of national well-being are changing, it might ultimately make possible a better evaluation of what public programs are accomplishing.

The existing situation in areas with which public policy must deal is often unclear, not only to the citizenry in general, but to officialdom as well. The normal processes of journalism and the observations of daily life do not allow a complete or balanced view of the condition of the society. Different problems have different degrees of visibility.

The visibility of a social problem can depend, for example, upon its "news value" or potential drama. The Nation's progress in the space race and the need for space research get a lot of publicity because of the adventure inherent in manned space exploration. Television and tabloid remind us almost daily of the problems of crime, drugs, riots, and sexual misadventure. The rate of infant mortality may be a good measure of the condition of a society, but this rate is rarely mentioned in the public press, or even percieved as a public problem. The experience of parents (or infants) does not insure that the problem of infant mortality is percieved as a social problem; only when we know that more than a dozen nations have lower rates of infant mortality than the United States can we begin to make a valid judgment about the condition of this aspect of American society.

Moreover, some groups in our society are well organized, but others are not. This means that the problems of some groups are articulated and advertised, whereas the problems of others are not. Public problems also differ in the extent to which they are immediately evident to the "naked eye." A natural disaster or overcrowding of the highways will be immediately obvious. But ineffectiveness of an educational system or the alienation of youth and minority groups is often evident only when it is too late.

Besides developing measures of the social conditions we care about we also need to see how these measures are changing in response to public programs. If we mount a major program to provide prenatal and maternity care for mothers, does infant mortality go down? If we channel new resources into special programs for educating poor children, does their performance in school eventually increase? If we mount a "war on poverty," what happens to the number of poor people? If we enact new regulations against the emission of pollutants, does pollution diminish?

These are not easy questions, since all major social problems are influenced by many things besides governmental action, and it is hard to disentangle the different effects of different causal factors. But at least in the long run evaluation of the effectiveness of public programs will be improved if we have social indicators to tell us how social conditions are changing.

The Contents of the Report

The present volume is not a social report. It is a step in the direction of a social report and the development of a comprehensive set of social indicators.

The report represents an attempt, on the part of social scientists, to look at several important areas and digest what is known about progress toward generally accepted goals. The areas treated in this way are health, social mobility, the condition of the physical environment, income and poverty, public order and safety, and learning, science, and art.

There is also a chapter on participation in social institutions, but because of the lack of measures of improvement or retrogression in this area, it aspires to do no more than pose important questions.

Even the chapters included leave many—perhaps most—questions unanswered. We have measures of death and illness, but no measures of physical vigor or mental health. We have measures of the level and distribution of income, but no measures of the satisfaction that income brings. We have measures of air and water pollution, but no way to tell whether our environment is, on balance, becoming uglier or more beautiful. We have some clues about the test performance of children, but no information about their creativity or attitude toward intellectual endeavor. We have often spoken of the condition of Negro Americans, but have not had the data needed to report on Hispanic Americans, American Indians, or other ethnic minorities.

If the Nation is to be able to do better social reporting in the future, and do justice to all of the problems that have not been treated here, it will need a wide variety of information that is not available now. It will need not only statistics on additional aspects of the condition of the Nation as a whole, but also information on different groups of Americans. It will need more data on the aged, on youth, and on women, as well as on ethnic minorities. It will need information not only on objective conditions, but also on how different groups of Americans perceive the conditions in which they find themselves.

We shall now summarize each of the chapters in turn.

Health and Illness

There have been dramatic increases in health and life expectancy in the twentieth century, but they have been mainly the result of developments whose immediate effect has been on the younger age groups. The expectancy of life at birth in the United States has increased from 47.3 years at the turn of the century to 70.5 years in 1967, or by well over 20 years. The number of expected years of life remaining at age 5 has increased by about 12 years, and that at age 25 about 9 years, but that at age 65 not even 3 years. Modern medicine and standards of living have evidently been able to do a great deal for the young, and especially the very young, but not so much for the old.

This dramatic improvement had slowed down by the early fifties. Since then it has been difficult to say whether our health and life status have been improving or not. Some diseases are becoming less common and others are becoming more common, and life expectancy has changed rather little. We can get some idea whether or not there has been improvement on balance by calculating the "expectancy of *healthy* life" (i.e., life expectancy free of bed-disability and institutionalization). The expectancy of healthy life at birth seems to have improved a trifle since 1957, the first year for which the needed data are available, but certainly not as much as the improvements in medical knowledge and standards of living might have led us to hope.

The American people have almost certainly not exploited all of the potential for better health inherent in existing medical knowledge and standards of living. This is suggested by the fact that Negro Americans have on the average about seven years less expectancy of healthy life than whites, and the fact that at least 15 nations have longer life expectancy at birth than we do.

Why are we not as healthy as we could be? Though our style of life (lack of exercise, smoking, stress, etc.) is partly responsible, there is evidence which strongly suggests that social and economic deprivation and the uneven distribution of medical care are a large part of the problem.

Though the passage of Medicare legislation has assured many older Americans that they can afford the medical care they need, the steps to improve the access to medical care for the young have been much less extensive.

The Nation's system of financing medical care also provides an incentive for the relative underuse of preventive, as opposed to curative and ameliorative, care. Medical insurance may reimburse a patient for the hospital care he gets, but rarely for the checkup that might have kept him well. Our system of relief for the medically indigent, and the fee-for-service method of physician payment, similarly provide no inducements for adequate preventive care.

The emphasis on curative care means that hospitals are sometimes used when some less intensive form of care would do as well. This overuse of hospitals is one of the factors responsible for the extraordinary increases in the price of hospital care.

Between June 1967 and June 1968, hospital daily service charges increased by 12 percent, and in the previous 12 months they increased by almost 22 percent. Physicians' fees have not increased as much—

they rose by 5½ percent between June 1967 and June 1968—but they still rose more than the general price level. Medical care prices in the aggregate rose at an annual rate of 6.5 percent during 1965–67.

Social Mobility

The belief that no individual should be denied the opportunity to better his condition because of the circumstances of his birth continues to be one of the foundation stones in the structure of American values. But is the actual degree of opportunity and social mobility as great now as it has been?

It was possible to get a partial answer to this question from a survey which asked a sample of American men about their fathers' usual occupations as well as about their own job characteristics. Estimates based on these data suggest that opportunity to rise to an occupation with a higher relative status has not been declining in recent years, and might even have increased slightly. They also show that by far the largest part of the variation in occupational status was explained by factors other than the occupation of the father.

These encouraging findings, in the face of many factors that everyday observation suggest must limit opportunity, are probably due in part to the expansion of educational opportunities. There is some tendency for the sons of those of high education and status to obtain more education than others (an extra year of schooling for the father means on the average an extra 0.3 or 0.4 of a year of education for the son), and this additional education brings somewhat higher occupational status on the average. However, the variations in education that are not explained by the socioeconomic status of the father, and the effects that these variations have on occupational status, are much larger. Thus, on balance, increased education seems to have increased opportunity and upward mobility.

There is one dramatic exception to the finding that opportunity is generally available. The opportunity of Negroes appears to be restricted to a very great extent by current race discrimination and other factors specifically related to race. Though it is true that the average adult Negro comes from a family with a lower socioeconomic status than the average white, and has had fewer years of schooling, and that these and other "background" factors reduce his income, it does not appear to be possible to explain anything like all of the difference in income between blacks and whites in terms of such background factors. After a variety of background factors that impair the qualifications of the average Negro are taken into account, there remains a difference in income of over $1,400 that is difficult to explain without reference to current discrimination. So is the fact that a high status Negro is less likely to be able to pass his status on to his son than is a high status white. A number of other studies tend to add to the evidence that there is continuing discrimination in employment, as does the relationship between Federal employment and contracts (with their equal opportunity provisions) and the above-average proportion of Negroes in high status jobs.

The implication of all this is that the American commitment to opportunity is within sight of being honored in the case of whites, but that it is very far indeed from being honored for the Negro. In addition to the handicaps that arise out of history and past discrimination, the Negro also continues to obtain less reward for his qualifications than he would if he were white.

The Physical Environment

This chapter deals with the pollution of the natural environment, and with the manmade, physical environment provided by our housing and the structure of our cities.

Pollution seems to be many problems in many places—air pollution in some communities, water pollution in others, automobile junk yards and other solid wastes in still other places. These seemingly disparate problems can be tied together by one basic fact: The total weight of materials taken into the economy from nature must equal the total weight of materials ultimately discharged as wastes plus any materials recycled.

This means that, given the level and composition of the resources used by the economy, and the degree of recycling, any reduction in one form of waste discharge must be ultimately accompanied by an increase in the discharge of some other kind of waste. For example, some air pollution can be prevented by washing out the particles—but this can mean water pollution, or alternatively solid wastes.

Since the economy does not destroy the matter it absorbs there will be a tendency for the pollution problem to increase with the growth of population and economic activity. In 1965 the transportation system in the United States produced 76 million tons of five major pollutants. If the transportation technology used does not greatly change, the problem of air pollution may be expected to rise with the growth in the number of automobiles, airplanes, and so on. Similarly, the industrial sector of the economy has been growing at about 4½ percent per year. This suggests that, if this rate of growth were to continue, industrial production would have increased ten-fold by the year 2020, and that in the absence of new methods and policies, industrial wastes would have risen by a like proportion.

The chapter presents some measures of air and water pollution indicating that unsatisfactorily high levels of pollution exist in many places. There can be little doubt that pollution is a significant problem already, and that this is an area in which, at least in the absence of timely reporting and intelligent policy, the condition of society can all too easily deteriorate.

As we shift perspective from the natural environment to the housing that shelters us from it, we see a more encouraging trend. The physical quality of the housing in the country is improving steadily, in city center and suburb alike. In 1960, 84 percent of the dwelling units in the country were described as "structurally sound;" in 1966, this percentage had risen to 90 percent. In center cities the percentage had risen from 80 percent in 1960 to 93 percent in 1966. In 1950, 16 percent of the nation's housing was "overcrowded" in the sense that it contained 1.01 or more persons per room. But by 1960, only 12 percent of the nation's housing supply was overcrowded by this standard.

The principal reason for this improvement was the increased per capita income and demand for housing. About 11½ million new housing units were started in the United States between 1960 and 1967, and the figures on the declining proportions of structurally unsound and overcrowded dwellings, even in central cities, suggest that this new construction increased the supply of housing available to people at all income levels.

Even though the housing stock is improving, racial segregation and other barriers keep many Americans from moving into the housing that is being built or vacated, and deny them a full share in the benefits of the improvement in the Nation's housing supply.

Income and Poverty

The Gross National Product in the United States is about $1,000 higher per person than that of Sweden, the second highest nation. In 1969 our GNP should exceed $900 billion. Personal income has quadrupled in this century, even after allowing for changes in population and the value of money.

Generally speaking, however, the distribution of income in the United States has remained practically unchanged over the last 20 years. Although the distribution of income has been relatively stable, the rise in income levels has meant that the number of persons below the poverty line has declined. The poor numbered 40 million in 1960 and 26 million in 1967.

A continuation of present trends, however, would by no means eliminate poverty. The principal cause of the decline has been an increase in earnings. But some of the poor are unable to work because they are too young, too old, disabled or otherwise prevented from doing so. They would not, therefore, be directly helped by increased levels of wages and earnings in the economy as a whole. Moreover, even the working poor will continue to account for a substantial number of persons by 1974: about 5 million by most recent estimates. This latter group is not now generally eligible for income supplementation.

The Nation's present system of income maintenance is badly in need of reform. It is inadequate to the needs of those who do receive aid and millions of persons are omitted altogether.

This chapter concludes with an analysis of existing programs and a discussion of new proposals which have been put forward in recent years as solutions to the welfare crisis.

Public Order and Safety

The concern about public order and safety in the United States is greater now than it has been in some time.

The compilations of the Federal Bureau of Investigation show an increase in major crimes of 13 percent in 1964, 6 percent in 1965, 11 percent in 1966, and 17 percent in 1967. And studies undertaken for the President's Crime Commission in 1965 indicate that several times as many crimes occur as are reported.

Crime is concentrated among the poor. Both its perpetrators and its victims are more likely to be residents of the poverty areas of central cities than of suburbs and rural areas. Many of those residents in the urban ghettoes are Negroes. Negroes have much higher arrest rates than whites, but it is less widely known that Negroes also have higher rates of victimization than whites of any income group.

Young people commit a disproportionate share of crimes. Part of the recent increase in crime rates can be attributed to the growing proportion of young people in the population. At the same time, the propensity of youth to commit crime appears to be increasing.

Fear of apprehension and punishment undoubtedly deters some crime. The crime rate in a neighborhood drops with much more intensive policing. But crime and disorder tend to center among young people in ghetto areas, where the prospects for legitimate and socially useful activity are poorest. It seems unlikely that harsher punishment, a strengthening of public prosecutors, or more police can, by themselves, prevent either individual crime or civil disorder. The objective opportunities for the poor, and their attitudes toward the police and the law, must also change before the problems can be solved.

Learning, Science, and Art

The state of the Nation depends to a great degree on how much our children learn, and on what our scientists and artists create. Learning, discovery, and creativity are not only valued in themselves, but are also resources that are important for the Nation's future.

In view of the importance of education, it might be supposed that there would be many assessments of what or how much American children learn. But this is not in fact the case. The standard sources of educational statistics give us hundreds of pages on the resources used for schooling, but almost no information at all on the extent to which these resources have achieved their purpose.

It is possible to get some insight into whether American children are learning more than children of the same age did earlier from a variety of achievement tests that are given throughout the country, mainly to judge individual students and classes. These tests suggest that there may have been a significant improvement in test score performance of children since the 1950's.

When the chapter turns to the learning and education of the poor and the disadvantaged, the results are less encouraging. Groups that suffer social and economic deprivation systematically learn less than those who have more comfortable backgrounds.

Even when they do as well on achievement tests, they are much less likely to go on to college. Of those high school seniors who are in the top one-fifth in terms of academic ability, 95 percent will ultimately go on to college if their parents are in the top socioeconomic quartile, but only half of the equally able students from the bottom socioeconomic quartile will attend college. Students from the top socioeconomic quartile are five times as likely to go to graduate school as comparably able students from the bottom socioeconomic quartile.

It is more difficult to assess the state of science and art than the learning of American youth. But two factors nonetheless emerge rather clearly. One is that American science is advancing at a most rapid rate, and appears to be doing very well in relation to other countries. The Nation's "technological balance of payments," for example, suggests that we have a considerable lead over other countries in technological know-how.

The other point that emerges with reasonable clarity is that, however vibrant the cultural life of the Nation may be, many of the live or performing arts are in financial difficulty. Since there is essentially no increase in productivity in live performances (it will always take four musicians for a quartet), and increasing productivity in the rest of the economy continually makes earnings in the society rise, the relative cost of live performances tends to go up steadily. This can be a significant public problem, at least in those cases where a large number of live performances is needed to insure that promising artists get the training and opportunity they need to realize their full potential.

Participation and Alienation: What We Need To Learn

Americans are concerned, not only about progress along the dimensions that have so far been described, but also about the special functions that our political and social institutions perform. It matters whether goals have been achieved in a democratic or a totalitarian way, and whether the group relationships in our society are harmonious and satisfying.

Unfortunately, the data on the performance of our political and social institutions are uniquely scanty. The chapter on "Participation and Alienation" cannot even hope to do much more than ask the right questions. But such questioning is also of use, for it can remind us of the range of considerations we should keep in mind when setting public policy, and encourage the collection of the needed data in the future.

Perhaps the most obvious function that we expect our institutions to perform is that of protecting our individual freedom. Individual liberty is not only important in itself, but also necessary to the viability of a democratic political system. Freedom can be abridged not only by government action, but also by the social and economic ostracism and discrimination that results from popular intolerance. There is accordingly a need for survey data that can discern any major changes in the degree of tolerance and in the willingness to state unpopular points of view, as well as information about the legal enforcement of constitutional guarantees.

Though liberty gives us the scope we need to achieve our individual purposes, it does not by itself satisfy the need for congenial social relationships and a sense of belonging. The chapter presents evidence which suggests (but does not prove) that at least many people not only enjoy, but also need, a clear sense of belonging, a feeling of attachment to some social group.

There is evidence for this conjecture in the relationship between family status, health, and death rates. In general, married people have lower age-adjusted death rates, lower rates of usage of facilities for the mentally ill, lower suicide rates, and probably also lower rates of alcoholism than those who have been widowed, divorced, or remained single. It is, of course, possible that those who are physically or mentally ill are less likely to find marriage partners, and that this explains part of the correlation. But the pattern of results, and especially the particularly high rates of those who are widowed, strongly suggest that this could not be the whole story.

There are also fragments of evidence which suggest that those who do not normally belong to voluntary organizations, cohesive neighborhoods, families, or other social groupings probably tend to have somewhat higher levels of "alienation" than other Americans.

Some surveys suggest that Negroes, and whites with high degrees of racial prejudice, are more likely to be alienated than other Americans. This, in turn, suggests that alienation has some importance for the cohesion of American society, and that the extent of group participation and the sense of community are important aspects of the condition of the Nation. If this is true, it follows that we need much more information about these aspects of the life of our society.

It is a basic precept of a democratic society that citizens should have equal rights in the political and organizational life of the society. Thus there is also a need for more and better information about the extent to which all Americans enjoy equality before the law, equal franchise, and fair access to public services and utilities. The growth of large scale, bureaucratic organizations, the difficulties many Americans (especially those with the least education and confidence) have in dealing with such organizations, and the resulting demands for democratic participation make the need for better information on this problem particularly urgent.

* * *

Though almost all Americans want progress along each of the dimensions of well being discussed in this Report, the Nation cannot make rapid progress along all of them at once. That would take more resources than we have. The Nation must decide which objectives should have the higher priorities, and choose the most efficient programs for attaining these objectives. Social reporting cannot make the hard choices the Nation must make any easier, but ultimately it can help to insure that they are not made in ignorance of the Nation's needs.

Chapter I

Health and Illness

ARE WE BECOMING HEALTHIER?

GOOD HEALTH and a long life are among the most elementary requirements for human achievement and enjoyment. The primary concern of this chapter is to review and appraise both the change in health and life expectancy among groups in our society and also the factors which have influenced the Nation's health status.

The satisfactions a positive state of health can bring are matters for other chapters. Even the extent of pain, worry, and discomfort due to poor health must be neglected because they cannot be measured at this time.

ARE WE GETTING HEALTHIER?

Long-Run Gains

The advance of medical science and rising standards of living in the twentieth century have brought about major improvements in health and life expectancy. Some diseases, like polio and diphtheria, have almost disappeared. Others, like tuberculosis and measles, are far less common than they used to be. The "miracle" drugs have reduced the danger from pnuemonia and other infectious diseases to an extraordinary degree.

The increase in life expectancy has been striking (table 1). At the turn of the century, the average life expectancy at birth in the United States was 49.2 years; in 1966, it was 70.1 years. Women have gained more than men. In 1900, women lived 2 years longer than men on the average; they now live 7 years longer.

TABLE 1.—*Average Number of Years of Life Remaining at Specified Ages: United States, 1900–02 and 1966*

Age at beginning of year	Average number of years of life remaining		Increase in average remaining lifetime (in years)
	1900–02	1966	
Birth	49.2	70.1	20.9
1	55.2	70.8	15.6
5	55.0	67.1	12.1
25	39.1	48.0	8.9
65	11.9	14.6	2.7

The gain in expectation of life at birth has occurred mainly because of the reduction in the death rates among infants and children. In 1900, the average child, age 5, could expect an additional 55 years of life; now a 5-year-old can expect to live an additional 67.1 years, or a gain of 12.1 years. In contrast, life expectancy among 25-year-olds has increased 8.9 years, and a typical 65-year-old can only expect another 2.7 years of life.

Life expectancy at older ages has not improved greatly because medical science has not yet developed the knowledge needed to control the degenerative diseases of old age. As more people survive long enough to become vulnerable to these diseases, death rates from the chronic, noninfectious diseases have continued to increase. In 1966, heart disease, cancer, and stroke accounted for two-thirds of all deaths, compared to less than 20 percent in 1920. (However, with the recent breakthrough in drug therapy for hypertension and Parkinson's disease, new knowledge is beginning to be brought to bear on some of the degenerative diseases of old age.) The incidence of some degenerative diseases that are painful or crippling, but usually not fatal, such as arthritis, has also increased.

Though all groups of Americans have come to have a longer life expectancy, some groups are still far behind others. Nonwhite expectation of life at birth in 1900 was 33.0 years, 14.6 years below that of whites. By 1965, nonwhite life expectancy had risen to 64.1 years but was still 6.9 years below that of whites. Though the risk of death in early childhood has decreased markedly for both white and nonwhite children, the disparity between the death rates for white and nonwhite children has actually increased over the years. In 1965, the nonwhite death rate for infants under one year of age was 187 percent of the white rate, as compared to 160 percent in 1935.

Some Recent Trends

Since the mid-fifties, there have been some gains in health, some losses, and some areas where we are holding our own or where progress has been uncertain. For example, the incidence of such infectious diseases as diphtheria, measles, polio, and whooping cough has declined since 1957. On the other hand, some diseases, including hepatitis, food-borne infections and streptococcal infections, have become more frequent. In addition, age-specific death rates for coronary heart disease among adults have continued to advance, as have death rates for cancer of the lung, cirrhosis of the liver, and chronic lung diseases such as emphysema and chronic bronchitis. The death rate from motor vehicle accidents has also risen but less markedly.

We can get an impression of what this mixed picture of gains and losses means on balance with the aid of a social indicator calculated for this Report. This is the "expectancy of *healthy* life" (or, more precisely, life expectancy free of bed-disability and institutional confinement). It takes into account any changes in the length of healthy life that are due to reductions in bed-disability or institutional confinement and also those that are due to increases in life expectancy. It reveals that the number of years of healthy life that Americans can look forward to has changed little since the late fifties, when the data on which this index is based first became available.

As table 2 shows, the unchanged life expectancy over the decade and the static expectation of disability days have resulted in a nearly constant expectation of healthy life. The figure in 1957–58 was 67.2 years, but this was a year of an influenza epidemic, so no upward trend can be clearly established, and if one exists at all it is very slight. The figures on expectation of healthy life remaining at age 65, shown in table 2, also indicate only limited improvement.

Males and females show slightly different patterns. Since 1958, females gained a full year of total life expectancy at birth or 1.3 years free of bed-disability, while males improved their situation by only 0.4 years of life expectancy or 0.6 years free of bed-disability. Expectations at age 65 show even greater sex discrepancies, with males having made no advances at all while females gained about a half year in both total and disability-free years.

The finding that expectation of healthy life is increasing so slowly does not necessarily mean that the health of the population has not improved. The measure of expectation of healthy life does not take into account differences in suffering. It is likely that the average day of bed-disability has become easier to bear in recent years because of the development of tranquilizers, pain killers, and sedatives. Also, the index does not measure any progress in relieving victims of the many illnesses that do not require bed disability. During July 1966–June 1967, the average American experienced 15.4 days of restricted activity, of which only 5.6 days involved bed-disability.

TABLE 2.—*Expectation of Healthy Life at Birth, United States, Fiscal Years 1958–66*
(*in years*)

Fiscal year	Expectation of life [1]	Expected bed-disability and institutionalization during life [1]	Expectation of healthy life
1958	69.5	2.3	67.2
1959	69.6	1.8	67.8
1960	69.9	2.0	67.9
1961	69.9	1.9	68.0
1962	70.2	2.1	68.1
1963	70.0	2.1	67.9
1964	69.9	2.0	67.9
1965	70.2	2.0	68.2
1966	70.2	2.0	68.2

[1] See footnote on continuation of table, page 4.

Expectation of Healthy Life at Age 65 (in years)

Fiscal year	Expectation of life [1]	Expected bed-disability and institutionalization [1]	Expectation of healthy life
1958	14.2	1.1	13.1
1959	14.3	1.0	13.3
1960	14.5	1.1	13.4
1961	14.4	1.1	13.3
1962	14.6	1.1	13.5
1963	14.4	1.1	13.3
1964	14.3	1.1	13.2
1965	14.6	1.1	13.5
1966	14.6	1.1	13.5

[1] Disability and institutionalization figures are given in terms of the fiscal year. Expectation of life figures are for the calendar year during which the fiscal year began.

SOURCE: Estimated from published and unpublished data obtained from the Censuses of 1950 and 1960, and from the Health Interview Survey and Vital Statistics Division of the National Center for Health Statistics.

Recent reductions in infant mortality offer some hope. Though the infant mortality rate was practically unchanged from 1950 to 1965, it decreased by more than 5 percent in 1966 and by another 5 percent in 1967. We cannot be certain about the causes of this possible trend, but the sudden reduction in infant mortality may well be related to the new Federal programs for maternal and infant care and family planning.

Trends in Mental Health and Illness

It is difficult to know with certainty whether mental illness represents an area of improvement or a growing problem. Because of still unsolved problems of psychiatric diagnosis, and because the types of behavior that are considered manifestations of mental illness change with our culture, no adequate measures of the mental health of a population have been developed. There is, accordingly, very little nationwide data on the prevalence of emotional disturbance in the general population.

Local surveys have been carried out in the United States to determine the prevalence of mental disorders, but their results do not lend themselves to comparison. Despite the lack of comparability among studies, each shows that sizeable proportions of the population studied suffer or have suffered from a mental disorder.[1]

Data on trends in mental health status are also limited. Only for the most serious and incapacitating forms of mental illness which require hospital care do the data allow any judgments about changes over time.

---

[1] To illustrate, three of these surveys carried out in different parts of the United States during the past 30 years suggested the following:

(1) 60 per 1,000 of the total population of an urban area were on the active rolls of mental hospitals or a large number of other health, welfare, social, educational and correctional agencies that provided services to persons with mental disorders;

(2) at least 70 per 1,000 of the population of a rural county would have been referred to a mental health clinic had one existed in the county;

(3) at least 100 per 1,000 of the noninstitutional population, all ages, of a major urban area were found to have a serious mental disorder.

Still, it is noteworthy that the number of persons in state and county long-term care mental hospitals has declined, from 559 thousand in 1955 to 401 thousand in 1968. These data probably reflect mainly the impact of tranquilizers and other new drugs and the wider availability of community-based care which have reduced the need for prolonged hospitalization of the mentally ill.

HOW MUCH HEALTHIER COULD WE BE?

Is it realistic to hope for major gains in health and life expectancy during the next decade? In the absence of extraordinary scientific breakthroughs in the treatment of degenerative diseases, the gains in expectation of life will not begin to match those achieved during the first half of this century. Even if all deaths below age 55 were eliminated, expectation of life at birth would increase only 6.5 years.

To what extent could we improve health or extend life with presently known bio-medical knowledge and technology? To obtain some insights into this question we can compare the health status of different groups in this country. Though the possibility of some genetic differences in health and life expectancy cannot be excluded, large group differences in health and life expectancy would probably indicate that we had not done all that we could in applying medical skills and resources to advance health and life. Such differences would also be of interest because of what they told us about the inequalities in our society.

Another way in which we can examine the question of whether we could be significantly healthier with present technology and resources is by comparing the life expectancy of the United States with that of other developed countries. Some differences may conceivably be due to climatic or genetic factors, but large differences could surely not be explained in this way.

Differences Within the United States

The data reveal striking differences among the regions and groups in our society. There are, for instance, substantial differences in life expectancy among the geographic regions of the country. For white males, life expectancy at birth in the South is about one-half year below that in the North and West. There is a difference of about 5 years in life expectancy at birth between those States with the best records and those with the worst. Moreover, the infant mortality rate is twice as great in the poorest State as in the best State, and the maternal mortality rate was four times as great. Infant mortality rates are also available by county. In the worst 10 percent of the counties the infant mortality rate in 1961–65 was about 21 per 1,000 live births more than in the best 10 percent of the counties.

There is a significant difference in health status between whites and nonwhites. Though bed-disability is only slightly greater for Negroes, there is a major disparity between the life expectancy of Negroes and whites at almost every age (table 3).

Negro infant mortality has been about four-fifths greater than that of whites. Though infant mortality for whites was 20.6 per 1000 live births in 1966, for nonwhites it was 38.7 per 1000. Negro maternal mortality has been about *four* times as great as the white rate (in 1965, 90.2 and 22.4 maternal deaths per 100,000 live births, respectively).

TABLE 3.—*Average Number of Years of Life Remaining at Selected Ages, by Color and Sex: United States, 1964*

Age	Males White	Males Nonwhite	Males Difference	Females White	Females Nonwhite	Females Difference
0	67.7	61.1	6.6	74.6	67.2	7.4
5	64.6	59.5	5.1	71.3	65.1	6.2
15	54.9	49.9	5.0	61.5	55.4	6.1
25	45.6	40.9	4.7	51.8	45.9	5.9
45	27.4	24.7	2.7	32.9	28.7	4.2
65	13.0	12.8	0.2	16.3	15.6	0.7
75	8.1	9.8	−1.7	9.6	11.1	−1.5

Negroes also have higher death rates for infectious diseases than whites, and higher death rates for certain tumors, such as cancer of the cervix. Since all of these death rates are subject to large reductions through more and better health services, the inequalities in the distribution of health services in our society are clearly an important factor accounting for these differences.

Furthermore, the available information indicates that illness causing limited activity is significantly higher for persons with low incomes, both black and white. For example, for males in the working age group 45–64, those with incomes of less than $2,000 have three and one-half times as many disability days as those in the over $7,000 income group.[1]

In addition, several studies have shown that less than half of the low-income children with chronic conditions, including mental and emotional disorders and hearing and vision defects, are under treatment. Yet two-thirds of these conditions could be prevented or corrected if the appropriate health services were available.

International Comparisons

At least 15 nations have a longer life expectancy at birth than the United States. Life expectancy in the leading countries, Holland, Sweden, and Norway, is about 3.5 years longer than it is in the United

---

[1] In comparing low and high income groups, it should be noted that one reason why persons may have low income is that they are ill.

States. At the start of the decade at least 27 countries had lower age-adjusted death rates for heart disease among males than the United States.

Part of the explanation for our relatively low rank in life expectancy in comparison with other developed nations is our style of life and the competitive pressures in our society. More than a dozen countries have lower rates of ulcers, diabetes, cirrhosis of the liver, hypertension without heart involvement, and accidents than we do. Our high automobile accident rate is probably due to the fact that we have more automobiles and use them more. The rates of death from diabetes and cirrhosis of the liver may be partly explained by the fact that we eat and drink more than some other peoples. The high rates of ulcers and hypertension may be part of the price we pay for our dynamic and competitive economy.

Some of the areas in which we lag behind could be affected by the amount and quality of health services available to our population. In 1964, the United States ranked fourteenth among the countries with the lowest infant mortality rates. Moreover, our relative rank with respect to infant mortality rates has progressively worsened in recent decades. In 1950 the United States ranked fifth; in 1955 we ranked eighth; and we fell to twelfth by 1960. While many other countries were making great progress in the reduction of infant mortality, the United States rate declined sluggishly. At least five countries also have better maternal mortality rates than the United States. Finally, our death rates from tuberculosis and pneumonia are far from the best.

WHY AREN'T WE HEALTHIER?

The United States cannot attribute the shortcomings of its health record to a lack of total expenditures for health services or to deficiencies in its supply of highly trained health manpower. The United States spends more on health services as a percentage of Gross National Product than any other country. And the proportion of GNP devoted to health care is rising rapidly. It increased from 4.6 percent in fiscal year 1950 to 6.5 percent in fiscal year 1968 or from $12.1 billion to $53.1 billion. When compared to the 13 countries with better infant mortality rates than the United States in 1964, we had the fourth highest ratio of both dentists and physicians to population, and the third highest ratio of professional nurses to population.

Nor can our poor showing compared to many other developed nations be blamed on the state of biomedical science and technology in this country. The United States spends considerably more on biomedical research than any other country. It is widely thought that we are the leading nation in biomedical science and technology.

Genetic and environmental factors could possibly help to explain why our health is not better. Indeed, it is possible that adverse environmental factors and changes in life styles have canceled out many of the more recent improvements in health services. The chapter on the Physical Environment shows that air pollution can be detrimental to health. This is also evident from the increase in death rates during periods when pollution is exceptionally severe. And a growing majority of Americans live in large metropolitan areas which are generally subject to concentrations of polluted air.

Perhaps more important than environmental factors, however, is the American style of life. For the vast majority of the population, health may be adversely affected by rich diet, smoking, lack of exercise, and the pressure of business and professional life. The high pressure of life may explain why the United States' male life expectancy is so much lower, even in relation to other countries, than its female life expectancy. For the underprivileged minority, bad health may reflect inadequate diet and ignorance about both proper preventive behavior and the value of early medical care, as well as unfavorable housing and sanitary conditions.

Of all these adverse factors, the health consequences of smoking have been perhaps best documented in recent years.[1] A wide variety of studies indicate that cigarette smoking leads to a substantial excess of deaths among those who smoke. It increases the risk of death from chronic bronchitis, pulmonary emphysema, heart disease, and lung cancer. Life expectancy for young men is reduced by an average of 8 years in "heavy" cigarette smokers, those who smoke over two packs a day, and by an average of 4 years among those who smoke less than one-half pack per day.

Style of life and physical environment do not account fully for the shortcomings in our health status. Two other factors, the unequal distribution of our medical care and the deprivation suffered by the Nation's poor and disadvantaged, are also major causes of these shortcomings.

Socioeconomic Deprivation and the Distribution of Medical Care

The lower a person's income is, the less often he sees a doctor. Whether we look at data on visits to physicians per year, or the interval since the last visit, or the use of a specialist's services, we see a clear, positive relationship between higher income and greater use of physicians' services. At the same time, there is more illness to be treated among low income than high income people.

The use of dentists also varies markedly with income. More than 20 percent of people in families with incomes under $3,000 have *never*

---

[1] See, for example: *The Health Consequences of Smoking,* 1968 Supplement, U.S. Public Health Service Publication No. 1969.

visited a dentist, as compared to 7.2 percent of those in families with incomes over $10,000.

There is further evidence of the unequal distribution of medical care, and its importance for our health status, in the provision of prenatal care. Though virtually all American babies are now delivered in hospitals, the expectant mother usually seeks out prenatal care on her own initiative and at her own expense. As a result, in most major cities, one-third to one-half of the women delivered in public hospitals have had no prenatal care. This is in sharp contrast to the practice in the Netherlands, for example, where infant mortality rates are among the lowest. There, nearly all expectant mothers get prenatal care, but a substantial proportion of the babies are delivered at home rather than in hospitals.

A person's race is also related to the likelihood that he will obtain medical care, even after adjusting for differences in incomes. Negroes at every income level use medical services less than whites. The number of physician visits per year for Negroes earning $10,000 or more, for example, was 4.3 in 1963–64 as compared to 5.1 for whites with similar incomes. This suggests that cultural and educational factors may also influence the use of health services, and that fewer health services may be available and accessible to Negroes.

The place a person lives has a major effect upon his access to medical care. For example, Mississippi has less than one-half as many physicians in relation to its population as New York, and only 58 percent as high a doctor/population ratio as the national average. Rural areas tend to have fewer doctors in relation to population than metropolitan areas (about 55 percent as many) whereas inner city ghetto areas have fewer doctors than middle class neighborhoods in the same cities. In general, States with low doctor/population ratios tend to have high infant and maternal mortality rates, a relatively high incidence of infectious diseases, and a shorter than average life expectancy.

The Cost of Medical Care

The uneven distribution of medical care in this country is due in part to the fact that medical care is becoming more costly, even in relation to other goods and services. Medical care prices have been rising faster than other prices throughout the postwar period. From 1946 to 1967, all consumer prices increased 2.6 percent annually while medical care prices increased at an annual rate of 3.9 percent. Moreover, in recent years the rise in medical care prices has accelerated. They increased at an annual rate of 6.5 percent during 1965–67.

Hospital daily service charges have been increasing faster than other medical care prices. They rose at an annual rate of 8.3 percent from 1946 to 1967. More recently, hospital daily service charges have increased sharply. During the two-year period 1965–1967, hospital charges rose about 16 percent per year. Physicians' charges increased at an average annual rate of 7.0 percent during the same two-year period.

The relatively rapid rise in medical care prices and increases in demand for services have resulted in an increase in the percentage of personal disposable income devoted to medical care (from 4.1% in 1950 to 5.9% in 1966). Even so, the public probably consumes fewer medical services than they would have if prices had risen less rapidly.

Fortunately, the proportion of the direct medical expenditures that are paid by private health insurance or public programs has been rising, and this has greatly reduced individual financial burdens. From 1950 to 1966, the proportion of personal health care expenditures met by "third party" payments (government, private health insurance and philanthropy) rose from 35 percent of the total to 50 percent. Still, there are millions under 65 without private health insurance who do not qualify for aid under Medicaid, and who are accordingly left to their own resources when illness strikes. Moreover, it is estimated that Medicare covers only about 35 percent of the total medical care expenses for those age 65 and older. Thus, despite the fact that public outlays for personal health services have risen from $7.9 billion in fiscal year 1966 to $15.7 billion in fiscal year 1968, even the medically indigent and those persons over age 65 must still pay for a substantial share of their own medical expenses.

Though low income families spend a higher percentage of their income for medical care than more affluent families, they spend less in absolute terms. This shows up most notably where preventive, as opposed to curative or ameliorative, care is concerned. During 1963–64, for instance, 54 percent of those persons under 17 years of age with family incomes in excess of $10,000 had at least one general physical examination, but only 16 percent of those persons under 17 years of age with family incomes of less than $2,000 had such a routine checkup. Generally, poor people fall farther behind high income people in their expenditures for physicians' and dentists' services, which are partly for preventive purposes, than for hospital care, which is largely designed to cure or ameliorate existing health problems.

In addition to the direct costs of medical care, there are the costs of the earned income foregone when a person is sick or obtaining medical care. For the family with the medical problem, as for the economy as a whole, these costs are considerable. In 1963, an estimated 6.2 million man-years were lost through illness, and 4.6 million of these would have been economically productive.

One estimate has placed the value of the labor lost for that year at $23.8 billion. Such an estimate can only be illustrative, for we cannot know what labor would be worth in a society without any health problems. But it does emphasize the point that the indirect costs of health problems are considerable, and that the burden of expenditures for medical care often falls on people whose incomes have been diminished because they could not work.

The System of Providing Health Care

Given the unmet health needs of our population and the rapidly increasing cost of medical care, the Nation can certainly not afford to waste its health resources. Yet our system of providing and financing medical care fosters inefficiency and waste in several ways.

First, our methods of paying for health care provide incentives to use too little preventive care, and relatively too much curative and ameliorative care. Both private and public insurance generally cover hospital and surgical care, but they rarely reimburse patients for physical checkups and other forms of preventive care. There is considerable evidence that, as a consequence, our prevailing forms of health insurance have some effect on the decisions of patients, and the advice of physicians to patients, to use surgical services. A number of studies indicate that surgical rates for such "elective" procedures as tonsillectomies, hysterectomies, and appendectomies are considerably higher for persons with hospital insurance.

Even those who have no insurance are induced to take relatively too much curative and ameliorative care and relatively too little preventive care. The Chinese in ancient times used to pay their doctors when the patient was well, but not when he was sick. This system of payment gives a doctor a strong incentive to provide preventive care, but our system does not. Health professionals are usually paid in accordance with the amount of care rendered, and therefore they have little financial incentive (but considerable ethical incentives) to avoid providing unnecessary care.

Second, prevailing insurance plans generally give the patient incentives to use the highest cost component of the health care system—the hospital—when less costly outpatient facilities or services might be equally satisfactory. The United States has more short-term hospital beds in relation to population than all but a few countries, and there is a good deal of evidence that hospitals are overused in this country. For example, a detailed study of the Kaiser Health Plan in California, which is a comprehensive prepaid health care plan providing a full range of health care services, showed that the age-adjusted utilization rates for Kaiser hospitals were more than 30 percent below the California average. Thus, the Kaiser Plan held its rise in hospital expenditures to 15 percent during 1950–65, as compared to a 50-percent increase for the country as a whole.

Third, the reimbursement of hospitals on the basis of costs provides no rewards for efficient operation. The Medicare and Medicaid hospital reimbursement formulas, based on "reasonable cost," and the formulas of most private insurance plans, make it easy for hospitals to "pass on" cost increases to third parties. At present, there are generally no reimbursement systems which make the level of income of hospitals depend upon the ability to operate effectively and thereby control costs.

Further, our system of independent hospitals and practitioners discourages *coordination* among the various elements responsible for providing medical care. This in turn leads to gaps in the type of care offered, a wasteful duplication of facilities and equipment, and considerable difficulty for many individuals in finding points of entry into our medical care system. However, there are some examples which show that a greater degree of coordination of health services is readily possible. In some areas of the country regional planning bodies have been effective in assuring that unneeded facilities are not constructed. Further, some group practice plans provide convenient access to care, the appropriate utilization of the skills of different medical specialists, and comprehensive care. The experimental federally supported neighborhood health care centers for the poor may, moreover, demonstrate that greater use of paramedical personnel outside of the hospital setting can work effectively in this country. Our present almost exclusive reliance on the physician for care outside the hospital is in sharp contrast to the extensive use of such personnel as visiting nurses and midwives in many foreign countries.

Finally, a factor that *may* help account for the high cost of medical care is the basically "small scale" of the health industry. Hospitals in the United States are generally small in comparison to those of Europe and, unlike foreign hospitals and U.S. commercial plants, are usually independently managed. The most striking example of small-scale production is, of course, the individual physician, especially the general practitioner. Although group practice is increasing, it is still unusual for moderate size groups of physicians to practice together and utilize common laboratory facilities and ancillary staff.

THE POLICY CHALLENGE

We have seen that the first half of the twentieth century saw extraordinary advances in health and life expectancy, but that the rate of advance has been slower in the fifties and sixties. In large part this slower rate of advance has been due to the fact that many of the most serious health problems of infants, children, and young adults had been solved by midcentury, and to the fact that it has not been possible to make many significant scientific breakthroughs in the treatment and prevention of degenerative diseases associated with the process of aging.

Nonetheless, the considerably longer life expectancy in some other countries, and the differences in health status among the different groups in our own country suggest that we could have better health and longer life, even without any new breakthroughs in medical science. There can be little doubt that appropriate public policy decisions can help to alleviate some of the factors adversely affecting the health status of our population. Public policy can aim to redress the imbalance in health resources, prevent and control harmful environmental factors, and even influence our thinking about those personal habits and forms of behavior which may prove detrimental to our health.

We have made some progress in the provision of health care for the young, in offering better preventive care, and in providing broader access to mental health facilities. The neighborhood health care centers of the Office of Economic Opportunity and the comunity mental health centers supported through the National Institute of Mental Health are examples of new public policy actions in these areas.

But much remains to be done. Many old but still unresolved public policy questions must be reexamined. The preceding discussion of the health status of our Nation suggests that these are *among* the most important issues that must be resolved:

—How much of our resources should be devoted to medical research for tomorrow and how much to provide services now?

—Can the Nation provide health services in a manner which will not discourage preventive care, and which will insure that *all persons* have access to health services which are reasonably comprehensive?

—How much of the Nation's health resources should be used to serve the elderly as opposed to young children and those in the prime of life?

—Can we find new ways to meet the challenge to the health status of the population posed by sharp increases in medical care costs?

—How can public policy redirect or control harmful practices which damage our environment, and alter personal habits and styles of life harmful to health, while still allowing organizations and individuals a satisfactory degree of freedom?

At present, we have no answers or only partial answers to these and other questions. America, in short, needs not only more effort, but also more debate and thought, if it is to realize the full potential for better health and longer life inherent in its advanced level of scientific and economic development.

Chapter II

Social Mobility

HOW MUCH OPPORTUNITY IS THERE?

"AMERICA MEANS OPPORTUNITY." So said Ralph Waldo Emerson over a hundred years ago. Ever since our Nation began, Americans, probably more than others, have believed that the individual should have the opportunity to achieve whatever his talents can bring. They have not enjoyed complete equality of opportunity, but a belief in greater equality of opportunity has always been a part of the American creed.

Thus any inventory of the state of American society must ask how much equality of opportunity we have, and whether there is more or less than there used to be. Complete equality of opportunity exists when the social and economic status a person has is determined by his own abilities and efforts rather than by the circumstances of his birth. If a person's family background or race, for example, affect his ability to "get ahead," then the ideal of equality of opportunity has not been realized.

An improvement throughout the society in the prospects for a high income, an advanced education, or a white collar job, however, does *not* necessarily mean greater *equality* of opportunity. Such improvements in "life chances" for the population as a whole are, of course, important, but they are largely the result of economic progress, which is considered in another chapter. Here, we focus instead on the extent to which a person's status, *relative* to that of others in his society, is determined by his ability and effort, rather than by his social origins. True equality of opportunity means that some families must fall in *relative* social or economic position if others rise. Indeed, many Americans might not want complete equality of opportunity with its extreme emphasis on individual talent, and some might question whether an aristocracy of ability is really preferable to an aristocracy of birth. A society in which the most capable people were always able to rise to positions of leadership, however fair this might seem, could prove intolerable to those who were condemned to failure because they lacked the particular talents valued in that culture. We must, then, temper our desire for more equality of opportunity with the realization that it may also be necessary for the successful and talented to share their good fortune with those less well endowed. But, in this chapter, these issues need not concern us unduly, for no matter how much equality of opportunity there may be in our Nation, most people want more than we now have.

To assess the degree of opportunity and measure its changes over time, we have to be able to determine a man's relative "position" in society, so that we can say whether he has risen or fallen in status. Though there is no one ideal measure of social and economic position, a man's occupation is probably the best single indicator of his socioeconomic level. Other characteristics, like high income, education, social standing, community influence, and membership in prestigious organizations, can also bring high socioeconomic status. The man of independent means and wide influence may have a high standing in his community even if he does not work at a job, and the man in a religious or ethnic minority may be denied access to prestigious organizations in spite of his career success. Thus occupational mobility is not a perfect indicator of social mobility, and we cannot be sure that there is more or less equality of opportunity just because a man's occupational position is more or less dependent on his family background than at some earlier point in our history. Yet changes in occupational mobility probably tell us as much about changes in social mobility as any other single measure we could use. All of the ingredients of a high status usually vary with occupation and are roughly measured by it. In a modern society like the United States, moreover, men are admired primarily for the work they do. Accordingly, in this chapter, we will measure the extent of opportunity by looking at changes in occupational status from one generation to the next, asking in particular how an individual's family background bears on his chances of success. Toward the end of the chapter, we will also consider how the color of a man's skin affects his position in our society (or at least his economic opportunities). In this first attempt toward a social report, it was not possible to consider other circumstances, such as sex, religion, or national origin, that may limit success in our society. The special problems facing some of these groups are also of great concern to the Nation and it is hoped that any future report can give greater attention to them.

HOW MUCH EQUALITY OF OPPORTUNITY IS THERE?

Earlier in American history, the possibility of moving to the frontier, with its lack of established social structure, was supposed to provide at least some degree of equality of opportunity. The opportunities of the unsettled frontier have vanished, and modern American society has on-going institutions, established families, and an emphasis on educational credentials that could limit equality of opportunity. A number of observers have been understandably concerned that the extent of equality of opportunity may be decreasing as the Nation's institutions become older and the demands of modern technology place those with an inadequate educational background under an ever greater disadvantage. Among sociologists there has been a debate on the question of whether class lines, as reflected by occupational mobility, have or have not been hardening in the last several decades.

In 1962, the Bureau of the Census conducted a survey of "Occupational Changes in a Generation" which has made it possible to estimate the present extent of opportunity in this country and whether or not there is more or less than there used to be. This survey asked a representative sample of American men not only about their own first occupation, income, education, and the like, but also about their father's usual occupation. A separate survey asked a cross section of the American public what degree of status they thought attached to each occupation, and these responses were used to derive a numerical status "score" (ranging from 0 to 96) for each of 446 detailed Census occupations.[1]

As a result of these two surveys, it is possible to compare the occupational score of each man surveyed in 1962 with the score his father had, and thereby see how much influence the father's relative socioeconomic position had on the ranking of his son. Since the men surveyed were of different ages, it is also possible to get some impression about whether equality of opportunity has been increasing or decreasing by comparing the father-son status relationship of the older men with that of the younger.

The Present State of Opportunity

An analysis of the survey results undertaken by Professors Dudley Duncan and Peter Blau shows that the occupational achievements of the sons were *not* in any large degree explained by the socioeconomic levels of their fathers. To be exact, only 16 percent of the variation in the occupational scores of the men surveyed in 1962 was explained by the father's occupational status.[2] If the data and analyses are correct, it follows that the remaining 84 percent of the variation in socioeconomic status among the sons was not related to the socioeconomic

---

[1] The survey provided prestige ratings for 45 occupations. Census information on the income and education within each occupation was used to assign scores to all other occupations. The procedure was to assume that the relationship between the socioeconomic status of an occupation and the general level of income and education in that occupation was similar to the relationship found to exist between these variables in the 45 occupations for which direct scores were available. It was also known that the relative prestige of various occupations changes very little over time, which made it possible to use the same scores to measure the occupational status of both fathers and sons.

[2] In the language of the statistician, the correlation coefficient relating the occupational scores of fathers and sons was .40.

status of their fathers. Since there is a probability that the men whose fathers were of high socioeconomic status had on the average somewhat more ability than those whose fathers had lower socioeconomic status, some relationship between status of father and son might be expected even in a society with perfect equality of opportunity. Accordingly, the findings, though extremely tentative, tend to suggest that there is a considerable degree of social mobility in America.[3]

Trends in Opportunity

There is also some reason to suppose that the degree of equality of opportunity has *not* been declining in recent decades. The oldest group of men surveyed were between 55 and 64 years of age in 1962, and the youngest between 25 and 34, so the oldest group of men held their first jobs about 30 years before the youngest. As table 1 shows,

TABLE 1.—*Degree of relationship* between father's occupation and respondent's first job for four age groups, men 25 to 64 years old*

Age (years) in March 1962	
25–34	.380
35–44	.377
45–54	.388
55–64	.384

*Correlation Coefficient.

SOURCE: Peter M. Blau and Otis D. Duncan, *The American Occupational Structure* (New York, John Wiley & Sons, 1967), p. 110.

the degree of relationship between the status of father and son is roughly the same for older and younger groups. The relationship appears to be slightly less for the two younger groups than for the two older groups, but it would be a mistake to attach significance to these small changes, and infer that social mobility is increasing. The conclusion should rather be that opportunity and social mobility have shown no tendency to decline.

It might seem that historical changes in the occupational structure, such as the increasing importance of white collar and other high status jobs, have invalidated the conclusions. But, in fact, the statistical analysis that was used tended to abstract from these changes, since it related the *relative*, not the absolute, occupational positions of the men in the two generations. As a result, such changes in occupational structure presumably could not account for the findings.

---

[3] Some Americans may also wonder whether there is more or less opportunity in the United States than in other parts of the world. At least one study has shown that occupational opportunity, as here measured, is about the same in all industrialized countries. Interestingly enough, however, there is evidence that long distance social mobility—that is, the ability to go from rags to riches in a single generation—is greater in the United States than elsewhere, so there does seem to be a grain of truth in the Horatio Alger myth.

There is, to be sure, the possibility of other shortcomings in the data or analysis that qualify or invalidate the conclusions. If the material wealth of the fathers of the men surveyed were known, and comparisons made with the wealth or income of the sons, the results might well have been less impressive, since material wealth is presumably easier to pass on from generation to generation than a given occupational status.

These and other qualifications notwithstanding, it is most encouraging that the relative socioeconomic status of the father has only a small influence on the relative socioeconomic status of the son, and that this influence is not increasing.

EDUCATION AND OPPORTUNITY

What accounts for the degree of social mobility that we enjoy? And the obstacles to opportunity that remain? Here education plays an important but uncertain role. Education is the principal route to a high status occupation, but it is not obvious whether, on balance, it promotes social mobility. As the subsequent chapter on Learning, Science, and Art shows, socioeconomic status influences not only access to higher levels of education, but also the motivation and capacity to learn. In part, then, education is a "transmission belt," whereby initial advantages stemming from the family are maintained for the fortunate, whereas initial disadavantages are perpetuated for the unfortunate. On the other hand, education allows some able people from low status families to rise to a higher relative position in the society. We must assess the extent to which education limits social mobility and also the extent to which it increases it, so that we can evaluate the effect of additional education on equality of opportunity and find educational policies that will further this objective. We look first at the evidence which tends to suggest that education is the means by which parents bequeath superior status to their children.

Education as a Barrier to Mobility

The average person born in this century received more years of schooling than his parents did. As table 2 shows, the average white male born between 1900 and 1934 (aged 35 to 69 in 1969) spent 11 years in school whereas his father who was educated at a much earlier point in time spent only about 8 years in school. But, whenever these men were born, the education they obtained depended to some extent on the education their father received. Thus, fathers who had above-average education for their day have tended to produce sons who were well-educated relative to their own contemporaries. Specifically, for every extra year of education the family head receives, the son tends to get an additional three-tenths or four-tenths of a year of education. It is also clear from table 2 that this relationship between the relative educational attainment of fathers and sons has not changed much since the turn of the century.

TABLE 2.—*Mean number of school years completed by native white males and by the heads of their families of orientation, and average relationship of respondent's to head's schooling, by age, for men in the civilian non-institutional population of the United States: March 1962*

Respondent's year of birth	Family head	Respondent	Average increase in respondent's schooling for each year completed by head
All, 1900–1934	7.9	11.0	.376
1900–1904	7.4	9.4	.401
1905–1909	7.4	10.1	.398
1910–1914	7.5	10.6	.333
1915–1919	7.8	11.1	.336
1920–1924	8.0	11.4	.368
1925–1929	8.3	11.8	.337
1930–1934	8.7	12.0	.366

SOURCE: Beverly Duncan, *Family Factors and School Dropout: 1920–1960*, Cooperative Research Project No. 2258, U.S. Office of Education (Ann Arbor: University of Michigan, 1965), tables 3-1 and 3-2. (Based on data collected by the Bureau of the Census in the Current Population Survey and supplementary questionnaire, "Occupational Changes in a Generation," March 1962.)

Evidently, one way in which high status parents can assure the future success of their children is by providing them with a better than average education. The influence of socioeconomic status on years of schooling is particularly notable where college and graduate education are concerned. This is true even after differences in academic ability have been taken into account, as can be shown by using previously unpublished data from *Project Talent*, and considering only those high school graduates who rank in the top one-fifth of the sample in academic aptitude. If the parents of these relatively able youth are from the top socioeconomic quartile, 82 percent of them will go on to college in the first year after high school graduation. But, if their parents come from the bottom socioeconomic quartile, *only 37 percent* will go on to college in the first year after high school graduation. As table 3 shows, even 5 years after high school graduation, by which time almost everyone who will ever enter college has done so, only 50 percent of these high ability but low status youth will have entered college, and by this time 95 percent of the comparable students from high status families will have entered college. High school graduates from the top socioeconomic quartile who are in the third ability group are more likely to enter college than even the top ability group from the bottom socioeconomic quartile.

Differences in attendance at graduate or professional schools are even more striking. Five years after high school graduation, those high school graduates in the top fifth by ability are *five times more likely to be in a graduate or professional school* if their parents were in the top socioeconomic quartile than if their parents were in the bottom socioeconomic quartile.

There is also, as the subsequent chapter on Learning, Science, and Art will show, a tendency for children from families of low socioeconomic status to perform less well on tests than other children even when they have spent the same number of years in school. This learning differential further accentuates the differences in the initial advantages of children from low and high status families.

How Education Promotes Equality of Opportunity

On the other side of the ledger, we know that there are many factors independent of family socioeconomic status which influence educational attainment, and in turn occupational achievement. These include native mental ability, personality traits, the influence of stimulating teachers, and the like. If educational attainment depends mostly on these and similar factors, it will promote social mobility, by allowing those with ability and ambition to rise to a higher socioeconomic level than their parents. If, on the other hand, education depends mainly on family status it may simply be the means by which successful parents bequeath social and economic advantages to their children.

TABLE 3.—*Entrance to college, by ability and socioeconomic status (within 5 years after high school graduation)*

	Socioeconomic status quartile	Number of high school graduates in group	Number who enter college	Talent Loss
Top ability group (100–80%)	1. High	203,000	192,000 (95%)	11,000 (5%)
	2.	153,000	120,000 (79%)	33,000 (21%)
	3.	122,000	82,000 (67%)	40,000 (33%)
	4. Low	60,000	30,000 (50%)	30,000 (50%)
Totals		538,000	424,000 (79%)	114,000 (21%)
Ability group two (80–60%)	1. High	130,000	109,000 (84%)	21,000 (16%)
	2.	143,000	90,000 (63%)	53,000 (37%)
	3.	148,000	78,000 (52%)	70,000 (48%)
	4. Low	94,000	34,000 (36%)	60,000 (64%)
Totals		515,000	311,000 (60%)	204,000 (40%)
Total (top 40%)		1,053,000	735,000 (70%)	318,000 (30%)
Abiilty group three (60–40%)	1. High	94,000	65,000 (69%)	29,000 (31%)
	2.	135,000	63,000 (46%)	72,000 (54%)
	3.	159,000	55,000 (34%)	104,000 (66%)
	4. Low	148,000	35,000 (24%)	113,000 (76%)
Totals		536,000	218,000 (41%)	318,000 (59%)
Subtotal (1–3 quintiles)		1,600,000	952,000 (60%)	648,000 (40%)

NOTE.—Entrance to College means degree-credit only.

SOURCE: The probabilities for these tables are derived from unpublished data from Project Talent, 5-year follow-up surveys cf the 1960 twelfth and eleventh grade high school students. The 1965–1966 High School Graduates (*Digest of Educational Statistics*, 1967 edition, Office of Education, U.S. GPO, table 65, "Number of public and nonpublic high school graduates, by sex and State: 1955–66") were then distributed according to the Project Talent probabilities.

A statistical analysis, using again the data from the survey of "Occupational Changes in a Generation," tells us something about the role which education plays in promoting social mobility. In this analysis, which is summarized graphically in figure II–1, family background is defined to include father's occupation and education, number of siblings, nativity of birth, color, region of birth, and region of residence. It is evident from figure 2 that some part of the variation in occupational achievement is accounted for by the family background factors we have just mentioned. This is largely because individuals born in favorable circumstances (for example, in well-educated, white families in the North) come to be better educated than those born in less favorable circumstances. But, to a great extent, the educational attainment of a child is due to factors that are independent of his family background, and this education, in turn, helps him achieve a higher occupational status even if he had a disadvantaged family background. Indeed, individual differences in educational attainment that are independent of family background explain more than half of the variation in occupational scores attributable to education.

We can then conclude that social background factors, though important determinants of educational and occupational achievements, are *not* as important as the other factors that influence educational attainment and thereby allow those of humble birth to rise to the more prestigious occupations. What might be called the democratic discovery of talent through universal education is quantitatively more important than the educational advantages children from high status families enjoy.

Education could, to be sure, do still more to equalize opportunity. If education depended less on family background than it now does then it would give children from families with a low socioeconomic position a still greater opportunity to rise to a higher level. If, for example, the chance to go on to college did not depend so much on the financial resources of one's family, education would enable many more to climb up the ladder of occupational success. Though education could contribute much more to equality of opportunity, the fact that it has already contributed a good deal may explain why we expect so much of it.

OPPORTUNITY AND RACE

There is one glaring exception to the encouraging conclusions we have drawn. The same data that show abundant opportunity for most Americans also show that Negroes have much less occupational mobility than whites. This can be seen by looking at table 4. This table shows the occupational distributions of men whose fathers were in the same occupation, and also distinguishes the occupational distributions of Negroes from all of the others surveyed in the study of "Occupational Changes in a Generation."

The table reveals a striking result: Most Negro men, *regardless of their fathers' occupations*, were working at unskilled or semiskilled jobs. Even if their fathers were in professional, managerial, or pro-

Figure II–1: Sources of Variation in Occupational Achievement, for Men 20-64 Years Old in Experienced Civilian Labor Force: March 1962.

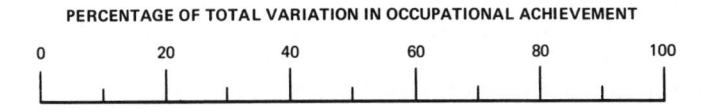

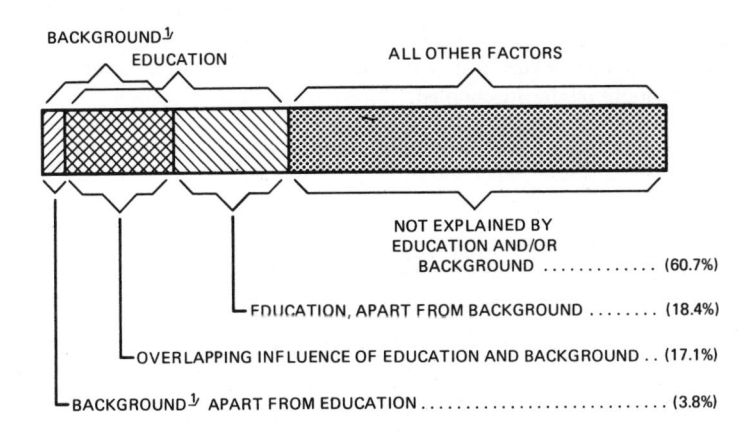

PERCENTAGE OF TOTAL VARIATION IN OCCUPATIONAL ACHIEVEMENT

BACKGROUND[1] EDUCATION   ALL OTHER FACTORS

NOT EXPLAINED BY EDUCATION AND/OR BACKGROUND .... (60.7%)

EDUCATION, APART FROM BACKGROUND .... (18.4%)

OVERLAPPING INFLUENCE OF EDUCATION AND BACKGROUND .. (17.1%)

BACKGROUND[1] APART FROM EDUCATION .... (3.8%)

TOTAL (100.0%)

Source: P.M. Blau and O.D. Duncan, *The American Occupational Structure*, (New York: Wiley, 1967), Appendix H.

[1] Background factors included:
- Family head's occupation
- Family head's education
- Number of siblings and sibling position
- Nativity
- Color
- Region of birth and region of residence

prietary positions, they were usually operatives, service workers, or laborers. Growing up in a family of high socioeconomic status was only a slight advantage for the Negro man. By contrast, the majority of white men with higher white collar backgrounds remained at their father's level and almost half of the white men whose fathers were in clerical or sales work and almost two-fifths of those with a farm or blue collar background moved up into the more prestigious professional and managerial group. But the Negroes from similar origins did not.

23

The Negro man originating at the lower levels is likely to stay there, the white man to move up. The Negro originating at the higher levels is likely to move down; the white man seldom does. The contrast is stark.

As we saw earlier in the chapter, education is an important source of occupational opportunity. Because most Americans can realize their highest ambitions through education, it is often assumed that Negroes can similarly overcome the handicaps of poverty and race. But this has not been so in the past. To be sure, even in minority groups, better educated individuals tend to occupy more desirable occupational positions than do the less educated. Yet the returns on an investment in education are much lower for Negroes than for the general population. Indeed, for a Negro, educational attainment may simply mean exposure to more severe and visible discrimination than is experienced by the dropout or the unschooled.

TABLE 4.—*Mobility from father's occupation to 1962 occupation (percentage distributions), by race, for civilian men 25 to 64 years old, March 1962*

Race and father's occupation	1962 Occupation [1]						Total	
	High white collar	Lower white collar	Higher manual	Lower manual	Farm	Not in experienced civilian labor force	Percent	Number (000)
Negro								
Higher white collar	10.4	9.7	19.4	53.0	0.0	7.5	100.0	134
Lower white collar	14.5	9.1	6.0	69.1	0.0	7.3	100.0	55
Higher manual	8.8	6.8	11.2	64.1	2.8	6.4	100.0	251
Lower manual	8.0	7.0	11.5	63.2	1.8	8.4	100.4	973
Farm	3.1	3.0	6.4	59.8	16.2	11.6	100.0	1,389
Not reported	2.4	6.5	11.1	65.9	3.1	11.1	100.0	712
Total, percent	5.2	5.4	9.5	62.2	7.7	10.0	100.0	
Total, number	182	190	334	2,184	272	352		3,514
Non-Negro								
Higher white collar	54.3	15.3	11.5	11.9	1.3	5.6	100.0	5,836
Lower white collar	45.1	18.3	13.5	14.6	1.5	7.1	100.0	2,652
Higher manual	28.1	11.8	27.9	24.0	1.0	7.3	100.0	6,512
Lower manual	21.3	11.5	22.5	36.0	1.7	6.9	100.0	8,798
Farm	16.5	7.0	19.8	28.8	20.4	7.5	100.0	9,991
Not reported	26.0	10.3	21.0	32.5	3.9	6.4	100.0	2,666
Total, percent	28.6	11.3	20.2	26.2	6.8	6.9	100.0	
Total, number	10,414	4,130	7,359	9,560	2,475	2,517		36,455

[1] Combinations of census major occupation groups. *Higher white collar:* professional and kindred workers, and managers, officials, and proprietors, except farm. *Lower white collar:* sales, clerical, and kindred workers. *Higher manual:* craftsmen, foremen, and kindred workers. *Lower manual:* operatives and kindred workers, service workers, and laborers, except farm. *Farm:* farmers and farm managers, farm laborers and foremen. Classification by "father's occupation" includes some men reporting on the occupation of a family head other than the father.

SOURCE: Unpublished tables, survey of "Occupational Changes in a Generation."

Thus, in addition to the handicap of being born in a family with few economic or other resources, the average Negro also appears to have less opportunity because of his race alone. Let us examine the relative importance of each of the different types of barriers to success for Negroes.

Figure 2 shows that the average Negro male completed 2.3 fewer years of school than the average white male, that his occupational score is 23.8 points lower, and that his income is $3,790 lower. Much of the shortfall in the relative achievement of Negroes can be attributed to specific causes. One year of the educational gap arises from the fact that Negroes come from disavantaged families while an additional 0.1 year is the result of the fact that Negroes tend to be born into larger families where resources must be spread among more children. But even with the allowance of 1.1 years of schooling traceable to these disadvantages, there remains an unexplained gap of 1.2 years. Evidently, this must be caused by something other than the initial socioeconomic differences between blacks and whites. Perhaps it is the Negro's knowledge that he will be discriminated against whatever his education.

FIGURE 2.—*Differences in means between white (W) and Negro (N) with respect to educational attainment, occupational status, and income, with components of differences generated by cumulative effects in a model of the socioeconomic life cycle, for native men, 25 to 64 years old, with nonfarm background and in the experienced civilian labor force: March 1962.*

Years of school completed	1962 occupation score	1961 income (dollars)	Component [1]
(W) 11.7 ⎤ 1.0 10.7 ⎤ 0.1 10.6 ⎤ 1.2 (N) 9.4 2.3	(W) 43.5 ⎤ 6.6 36.9 ⎤ 0.6 36.3 ⎤ 4.8 31.5 ⎤ 11.8 (N) 19.7 23.8	(W) 7,070 ⎤ 940 6,130 ⎤ 70 6,060 ⎤ 520 5,540 ⎤ 830 4,710 ⎤ 1,430 (N) 3,280 ⎤ 3,790	(A) [Family] (B) [Siblings] (C) [Education] (D) [Occupation] (E) [Income] (T) [Total]

[1] Difference due to:
(A) Socioeconomic level of family of origin (head's education and occupation).
(B) Number of siblings, net of family origin level.
(C) Education, net of siblings and family origin level.
(D) Occupation, net of education, siblings, and family origin level.
(E) Income, net of occupation, education, siblings, and family origin level.
(T) Total difference, (W) minus (N)=sum of components (A) through (E).

SOURCE: O. D. Duncan, "Inheritance of Poverty or Inheritance of Race?" forthcoming.

If we look at the *occupational gap* of 23.8 points, we see that 6.6 points can be ascribed to initial Negro-white differences in family socioeconomic levels and an additional 0.6 to differences in family size. The residual educational gap, already identified, carries over into occupational achievement, lowering the Negro score relative to the white by 4.8 points on the average. There remains a gap, not otherwise accounted for, of 11.8 points. This discrepancy derives from the fact that Negro men with the same schooling and the same family background as a comparable group of white men will have jobs of appreciably lower status. It is surely attributable in part to racial discrimination in hiring, promotion, and other job-related opportunities.

All of the factors mentioned are converted into an *income gap* totaling $3,790. Substantial components of this are due to socioeconomic status and family size ($1,010), lower educational attainment ($520), and job discrimination ($830), so that disadvantages detectable at earlier stages clearly have an important impact in lowering Negro income compared to white income. But there remains a gap of $1,430 not otherwise accounted for, suggesting that Negro men, relative to a group of white men of comparable family background, educational attainment, and occupational level, still receive much lower wages and salaries. The specific magnitudes obtained in calculations of this kind are not to be taken as firm estimates. Nevertheless, the substantial discrepancies existing between Negro and white attainment suggest that the Negro has severely limited opportunity, not only because his social and economic background place him at a disadvantage, but also because he faces racial discrimination in the school system and in the job market.

What can we conclude about social mobility in America? We have seen that there is opportunity for the great majority of our citizens to improve their relative occupational status through their own efforts. Yet we are far from achieving true equality of opportunity. Economic and social status in our society still depend in a striking way on the color of a man's skin. Until we can eliminate this barrier to full participation, we will not have been faithful to our historic ideals.

Chapter III

Our Physical Environment

ARE CONDITIONS IMPROVING?

IN THIS CHAPTER we are concerned with our physical surroundings: with the air we breathe, the water we use, the housing we occupy, the landscapes we see, and the transportation systems and urban patterns that determine the spatial dimensions of our lives.

THE NATURAL ENVIRONMENT

The natural environment is different for each community. In one community the air is polluted, but the water is reasonably clean; in another the reverse may be true. In a third place solid wastes—expanding graveyards of abandoned cars, or piles of trash—may be the most serious problems. In one place problems are getting worse; in another they are getting better. Programs designed to deal with pollution are as diverse as the problems themselves. Air, water, and land pollution are treated as separate and independent problems; the two Federal agencies with primary responsibilities for air and water pollution are in separate cabinet departments. Many State and local agencies also deal with one pollution problem or another.

To summarize the vast variety of environmental problems and policies we need to consider the interdependence of air, water, and land pollution, and the level and composition of the National Income. The "materials balance" framework provides an approach which can enable us to do this.

The Materials Balance Framework

We start with the fact that the total weight of materials taken into the economy from nature must ultimately equal the total weight of the wastes discharged, plus any materials recycled. This means that a reduction in any one kind of waste, such as particulate matter into the atmosphere, must be accompanied by an increase in some other kind of waste, such as dry solids or solids discharged into waterways, or else by a continual recycling of this material. Except for respiratory carbon dioxide and water, it is technologically possible to stop most of the present discharge of wastes into the air and watersheds. But the result would be an accumulation of solid wastes that might be equally objectionable.

The economy uses almost 1.5 billion tons of fuel each year.[1] The main products of combustion are gaseous oxides of carbon, hydrogen, sulfur, and nitrogen. These plus a portion of the solid ash are normally discharged into the atmosphere. The economy also takes in about another billion tons of minerals and food and forest products. Consumers use these goods in the form they receive them, or further transform them (e.g., by eating), but must sooner or later dispose of the end product, whether it be empty tin cans, "throw-away" bottles, worn-out refrigerators, plastic toys or human excreta.

Thus we can see that the pollution problem will probably increase as the economy grows. If, for example, industrial production tends to grow at 4½ percent per year, it will have increased fourfold by the year 2000 and almost tenfold by 2020. Unless there are changes in technology or the composition of output, the total weight of materials going through the economy, and the wastes generated, will have increased by a like amount. Surely this will not be allowed to happen. The society must continuously recycle more of the materials it uses, or reduce pollution in some other way. Still, this hypothetical projection alerts us to the fact that a new type of natural resource scarcity is emerging.

Since Malthus' time, the possibility of resource scarcity has held the attention of economists and laymen alike. Available evidence today suggests, however, that resource scarcity has not posed a threat to American economic growth over the last 60 years, nor is it likely to over the next 50 years.

The same cannot be said of the new type of scarcity: nature's limited capacity to absorb wastes. The present levels of pollution are serious enough. But unless we develop new technologies of recycling, they could become much worse.

We cannot draw any direct lines from the amount of wastes discharged in an area to the damage done by pollution. Some wastes, such as carbon dioxide, are not usually considered pollutants. In some areas, especially rural areas, the level of pollution may be below the threshold at which it begins to do damage. It is also possible that some parts of the environment can specialize as receivers of waste. Certain land areas and rivers could be loaded with wastes almost without limit, and

---

[1] This and the following estimates are from Ayres and Kneese, "Environmental Pollution," *Federal Programs for the Development of Human Resources*, A Compendium of Papers Submitted to the Subcommittee on Economic Progress of the Joint Economic Committee, Congress of the United States, 1968.

other areas and rivers kept in good condition for other uses. We must therefore look at each type of pollution in turn, along with its sources, effects, and geographic dispersion.

Air Pollution

In most of our large cities today more wastes are being discharged into the atmosphere than can be dissipated. The result is air pollution. Polluted air can contribute to sickness, disability, and premature death; it can soil and damage buildings and materials of all kinds; it can injure and destroy farm crops and other vegetation; and it can blight our cities and degrade the quality of our lives. In addition, the more distant future holds the ominous possibility of radical changes in climatic conditions.

a. Major Pollutants and Their Adverse Effects

Carbon monoxide is the most important air pollutant in terms of weight emitted into the atmosphere. Generated principally from transport vehicles and combustion processes, it can cause physical and mental impairment, and death.

Oxides of nitrogen and hydrocarbons (from autos and industrial sources) photochemically react to produce photochemical smog, the most irritating effect of which is eye irritation. Smog makes breathing more difficult, especially for those with respiratory diseases, and it has been known to cause serious plant damage.

Sulfur dioxide, from burning of coal and oil, damages vegetation, affects the lungs adversely, and has been associated with an increase in respiratory death rates and cardiovascular ailments among older persons. Sulfur trioxide, from the same source, converts to sulfuric acid in the air and causes corrosion and deterioration of certain fabrics and of steel and stone structures.

Particulate matter, such as lead from auto exhausts, may be directly harmful to human beings. Other particulates may magnify the adverse effects of other pollutants on the lungs, and soil structures and materials. Major sources are ash products of combustion in electric power and industrial production.

b. Air Pollution Levels

Are the levels of air pollution high enough in major American cities to create serious problems? Some idea of the significance of the air pollution problem can be obtained by comparing the actual levels of each type of pollutant in various cities with some standards for air quality, to see if air pollution exceeds an acceptable level.

It should be emphasized here that the best presently available information on air pollution problems is incomplete—hence the tentative nature of the goals. Because of the dire consequences of continued increases in pollution we have to take precautionary measures in the face of information which is not only insufficient but subject to change as our knowledge grows.

Two different sets of tentative air quality goals have been adopted. If the "tentative short range goals" were achieved, most of the undesirable effects now understood would be eliminated. The long range goals set more rigorous standards, since not all of the effects of air pollutants are known, and there is evidence which suggests that still lower levels must be reached to eliminate all of their detrimental effects.

An index of air pollution can be obtained by comparing a city's maximum pollution levels to the tentative air quality standards. There are six major American cities for which the index exists. None of the six cities meets even the tentative short range standards, suggesting that the air pollution problem is quite significant. A comparison of the maximum air pollution levels of the six cities with the long range standards indicates an even worse situation.

TABLE 1.—*Air Pollution Index (1 is barely adequate air; the higher the number the greater the pollution)*

	Based on tentative short range standards
Chicago	2.7
Los Angeles	2.2
Philadelphia	2.2
Washington	1.6
Cincinnati	1.6
San Francisco	1.1

On the basis of less detailed information, the National Center for Air Pollution Control (NCAPC) has ranked 65 metropolitan areas in order of the seriousness of their air pollution problems. The ten with the most serious problems are, in order:

1. New York
2. Chicago
3. Philadelphia
4. LA–Long Beach
5. Cleveland
6. Pittsburgh
7. Boston
8. Newark
9. Detroit
10. St. Louis

A glance at the major sources of air pollution makes it evident that substantial reductions in air pollution will not be easy. The NCAPC has estimated that energy conversion in the transportation system is the source of nearly 60 percent of all the major air pollutants, and 90 percent of the carbon monoxide. This suggests that a major reduction in the extent of air pollution would require either a substantial limitation in the use of the automobile, or else a type of automobile (like a steam or electric car) capable of generating less pollution.

Less radical and costly changes—such as smaller cars or more extensive use of trains—could, however, make a significant contribution. So would more emission control measures in industry and public utilities. Industrial sources account for 18 percent of all pollutants, and utilities and other energy conversion for another 21 percent. In the case of particulate matter resulting from electric power generation, for example, it has been estimated that rates of emission could be reduced by 80 percent by the year 2000 at a cost of $11 million per year, which is quite small in relation to total production cost.

Water Pollution

Water, like air, is often used as a waste receptacle. The accumulation of wastes that cannot be dissipated leads to pollution. The uses of water are more numerous and the relationships more complex than for air. Water which is too polluted to swim in may not be too polluted for fish. Water too polluted for fish may still be suitable for sailing or hydro-electric power generation. The uses of water must accordingly be taken into account before the severity of water pollution can be judged.

In recent years the use of water for recreational purposes has become more important. But the dumping of industrial wastes and municipal sewage into the Nation's waterways has diminished their ability to serve the rising demand for recreational facilities, which require higher water quality. It is necessary, therefore, not simply to maintain but to raise water quality.

The most common standard by which the quality of water is judged is the quantity of dissolved oxygen (d.o.) in it. When considerable quantities of organic materials are dumped into a river, the oxygen-using bacteria in these wastes draw down the level of dissolved oxygen. Since oxygen is necessary to support all forms of animal life, plankton and higher orders of animal life in the food chain, including fish, disappear. The depletion of oxygen also ultimately keeps the oxygen-using bacteria from decomposing the organic substances in the water into their basic chemical constituents, and a septic situation develops. Anerobic or non-oxygen using processes continue to bring about some decomposition of wastes, but these processes produce foul smelling gases.

Though they do not usually cause disease themselves, the presence of those forms of coliform bacteria normally found in the feces of warmblooded animals, including humans, indicates that there is a serious danger of harmful organisms in water. Thus the concentration of fecal coliforms, which normally come from municipal sewerage, is another measure of water quality. So is the concentration of synthetic organic compounds (from detergents), toxic substances (from herbicides and pesticides), plant nutrients, and specific industrial wastes, such as sediment, dissolved solids, and radioactivity. Industrial processes, and especially the generation of nuclear power, can also cause "thermal pollution" by heating the water and thereby harming fish. The acid drainages resulting from coal mining also make water unsuitable for fish or drinking, yet may make water clearer and more attractive and enhance its usefulness for some industrial purposes.

Some standards for water quality have been determined by a Technical Advisory Committee convened in 1967 to advise the Secretary of the Interior. This committee took account of both recreational and industrial uses, and the danger of polluted water to health. It established different standards of quality for different water uses.

These criteria can be compared with actual measurements of quality to determine where and how often water pollution forecloses certain uses of water. A sample of 25 stations in the Federal surveillance system was drawn, and the levels of dissolved oxygen and fecal coliforms observed. Seventeen of the stations reported at least one reading below the dissolved oxygen standard needed for fish and wildlife, and nine stations experienced such a condition more than 5 percent of the time. All of the stations observed had maximum coliform counts above the standard for general recreation use and public water supplies, and 10 had *average* counts above this standard. The Missouri-Mississippi Basin and the Cuyahoga, Sacramento, Delaware, and Potomac Rivers were unsafe even for boating more than 70 percent of the time. Thus, it appears that many major rivers are in appalling condition much of the time. On the other hand many rivers, particularly in the West, are relatively free of pollution.

The primary sources of water pollution are municipal and industrial wastes. The households of about 125 million people, or almost 90 percent of the urban population, are connected to sewer systems. Manufacturing wastes are also discharged through the same sewers and produce an organic waste load three times as great as households. Industrial wastes are probably responsible for a substantial part of the water pollution problem.

The extent of treatment of manufacturing wastes is not known, but we do know that sewer systems serving about 104 million people treat the wastes before they are discharged. About three-fifths of these, in turn, have both "primary" and "secondary" treatment, which removes at least 85 percent of the biological oxygen demand of the wastes.

If all municipal wastes were treated and if the effectiveness of treatment were raised to 85 percent, on average, actual municipal discharges into rivers would still be greater in 1980 than they were in 1962, and would have doubled by 2020. If, on the other hand, we raised the effectiveness of all treatment to 95 percent, municipal waste discharges into rivers would probably decline over the next 60 years. But 95 percent treatment goes to the outer limits of present technology, and would perhaps triple or quadruple treatment costs.

One estimate puts the costs of building and operating treatment plants that would remove at least 85 percent of the organic wastes from both municipal and industrial effluents by 1973 at over $20 billion, or $4 to $6 billion a year.

Pollution of the Land

Solid wastes are increasing both in variety and in volume. They include, in addition to garbage and ashes, considerable quantities of industrial wastes, old appliances, construction refuse, junked cars, agricultural chemicals, "throw away" cans, bottles, or plastic containers, and even radioactive materials. In an earlier period solid wastes were mainly organic materials that would be degraded over time, but they are now about 65 percent inorganic solids.

In 1966, the Nation disposed of an estimated 165 million tons of solid wastes. This total is expected to grow to about 265 million tons in 1976. Household wastes alone are considerable. Data in the late fifties showed that several cities collected close to four pounds of refuse per capita per day, and this level has since increased. In 1965, the Nation also disposed of about 6 to 6½ million motor vehicles. The burden of junked automobiles is, however, lessened by the fact that much of the material can be profitably reused; in 1965, about 15 percent of the rubber, and at least 90 percent of the steel was recovered from junked automobiles.

The accumulation of solid wastes has almost exhausted convenient landfills in many urban areas.[2] Solid wastes can be transported to rural areas, though at increasing cost. Landfills can also be used to reclaim swamps and marshes for urban uses, although there is evidence that this may have adverse effects on marine life. Filling coastal marshlands also appears to have an impact on fisheries which is not yet properly understood or measured.

Solid wastes also can be (and often are) incinerated, composted, or barged to the sea. This can increase air and water pollution. Indeed, the incineration of certain types of plastics found in solid wastes (especially Teflon, and fluorinated and vinyl plastics) produces chemical contaminants whose physiological effects may be similar to those of phosgene gas, a severe respiratory irritant used in World War I.

The costs of disposing of solid wastes are often considerable. Ayres and Kneese estimated that local governments spend about a billion and a half dollars on collecting and disposing of such wastes. Schools and

---

[2] *A Strategy for a Liveable Environment.* Report to the Secretary of HEW by the Task Force on Environmental Health and Related Problems, June 1967.

roads are the only items on which local governments spend more. These costs vary considerably with the level of service provided. A study of refuse collection in St. Louis showed that changing the pickups from the curb to the house doubled costs, and that an increase from two to three pickups a week increased costs by almost a third.[3]

The costs of different methods of disposal and locations for dumps are particularly crucial. Even with present technology, it is possible to prevent great damage to the quality of the environment, if only by hauling the wastes to uninhabited areas. But measures that completely protect the quality of the environment may be so costly they are not worthwhile. A wise policy concerning solid wastes must therefore be based on informed judgments about the benefits and costs of the relevant alternatives in each local situation.

Other Environmental Hazards

Some problems of the natural environment cannot be described in terms of the flow of materials through the economy. This is true of floods, droughts, erosion, hurricanes, and other natural hazards. Increased meteorological knowledge, better transportation and communication, new dams, irrigation works, and drainage systems, and better housing have greatly eased the problem of such natural disasters. Because of these and other protective measures, more people are able to live in disaster-prone areas. However, this tends to increase the population at risk to natural disasters.

Another environmental problem is noise. Noise is not only unpleasant and disruptive, but can also be a threat to health. Clinical evidence shows conclusively that noise can damage hearing. It has been estimated that more than 6 million Americans are subjected to hazardous noise levels at their jobs. Current levels of electronic amplification of music have also been shown to lead to at least temporary impairment of hearing. With increased crowding, electronic amplification of sound, use of machinery, sonic booms and other noises from the transportation system, the average noise level rises each year.

Outdoor Recreation

The natural environment is a source of esthetic satisfaction and the setting for outdoor recreation. Vast rural areas are almost totally unspoiled, and even some areas with significant pollution problems can be used for outdoor recreation.

Outdoor recreation is accordingly enjoyed on a wide scale. The Bureau of Outdoor Recreation has estimated the total number of "occasions" of outdoor recreation at 6.5 billion in 1965, or up 50 percent from 1960. This figure is expected to rise to 10 billion by 1980.

---

[3] Werner Hirsch, "Cost Functions of an Urban Government; Refuse Collection," *The Review of Economics and Statistics* (1965).

The forms of outdoor activity that attract the greatest number of people are walking for pleasure, swimming, picnics, and pleasure driving.

In 1965 there were some 345 million acres of designated rural recreation lands administered by Federal, State, and local agencies, or about 1.8 acres per capita. The Mountain States have 20,000 acres of such land per person, but New Jersey has only .06 acre per person.

The Bureau of Outdoor Recreation has indicated that outdoor recreation rises with income. This suggests that the extremely unequal distribution of public recreation land is a problem, and that the demand for outdoor recreation can be expected to increase as incomes rise.

THE MANMADE ENVIRONMENT

The quality of life obviously depends on the places we live in—our homes and communities.

a. THE QUANTITY AND QUALITY OF HOUSING

When high- or middle-income families build new homes at a faster rate than that at which the population grows, this tends to improve housing for low income people as well. The housing that is vacated by those who move into the new housing is usually sold or rented to families with lower incomes, and the housing these families occupied is usually then taken up by families with still lower incomes. We shall see that this procss has led to better housing for Americans at all income levels, but that some Americans have been denied the full benefits of the increase in the housing supply.

The quality of housing has improved substantially in recent years. The 1950 census revealed that 39 percent of the Nation's occupied housing failed to meet minimum standards, in the sense that it was either "dilapidated" or "deteriorating," or lacked adequate plumbing facilities. By 1960 only 16 percent, and by 1966 only 10 percent, of the Nation's housing failed to meet those standards.

Suburban areas had the lowest percentage of inadequate units with center cities second and nonmetropolitan areas the highest. The reduction in the amount of unsatisfactory housing was greatest in nonmetropolitan areas, next greatest in city centers, and least in the suburbs. The improvement, in other words, was greatest in the areas where the need was greatest.

The proportion of overcrowded housing has also declined. In 1950, 16 percent of the housing units were overcrowded, i.e., contained 1.01 or more persons per room. In 1960 the percentage of overcrowded units by this standard had fallen to 12 percent.

Admittedly, the change in the proportion of Americans with substandard or overcrowded housing is in some respects misleading. The minimal standards are too low to have any meaning for the average American, whose housing has exceeded the standards for some time. The unchanging standards also ignore the rising expectations that accompany the Nation's rising standard of living. Still, they do fairly reveal a substantial absolute improvement in the quality of housing for most of those who have lived in the poorest housing.

b. Causes of the Improvement

The principal reason for improvement is the construction of new housing, most of which has apparently been built for middle and upper income families. Between 1960 and 1967, 11.5 million new housing units were started in the United States. Of these, 98 percent were privately owned and 2 percent publicly owned. As was pointed out earlier, new housing construction has helped to elevate the quality of housing available to all.

Urban renewal has provided better housing for some poor families, but its effect has been slight. From the inception of the 1949 housing act through fiscal 1967, urban renewal provided only 107,000 new and 75,000 rehabilitated housing units. Urban renewal projects usually take from 6 to 9 years to complete.[4] As of July 1967, the urban renewal program had demolished 383,000 dwelling units, or more than it had built and rehabilitated. This is due in part to the fact that new construction in many of the urban renewal areas is not yet complete. Urban renewal efforts have not, in any case, been generally designed to add to the housing of the very poor. Of the new units built in urban renewal projects, only 10 percent were low rent public housing. Most of the 636,000 low rent federally administered housing units in existence at the end of 1966 were outside of urban renewal projects. These 636,000 housing units, though dwarfed by the size of the increase in new private housing, have nonetheless made a very important contribution to the housing of the poor.

c. Barriers and Inequities in the Housing Market

Unnecessary barriers and inequities have denied many Americans a fair share of the gain from the increase in the supply of good housing. A lack of access to credit, ignorance of available housing, zoning laws, and above all racial segregation have put many Americans at a disadvantage in the housing market, and limited the extent to which the construction of new housing has added to the housing available to them. Racial segregation in housing, for example, makes it difficult for Negroes to obtain new houses in the suburbs or even the housing vacated by others within the city. Most of the increased housing sup-

---

[4] This estimate was made by staff members of the National Commission on Urban Problems. See Anthony Downs, "Moving Toward Realistic Housing Goals," in *Agenda for the Nation*, Kermit Gordon, ed. (Washington: The Brookings Institution, 1968), pp. 141–178.

ply is reserved for whites, and blacks are left to compete for such housing as exists in the ghetto. Zoning laws which prohibit apartments, or houses on small lots, can similarly restrict the supply of housing of a kind that the poor can afford.

The importance of these barriers in the case of the Negro is clear. There is an almost total segregation of Negroes in most American cities. Table 2 shows that more than 85 percent of the Negroes in 109 cities would have to move from the block in which they live in order to achieve a random distribution of Negroes and whites over the entire metropolitan area.

The extent of segregation, moreover, is apparently not decreasing. As table 2 reveals, segregation has probably even increased from 1950 to 1960, because of the considerable increase in urban segregation in the South. The exact extent of housing segregation since the 1960 census is not known, but studies conducted since then suggest that there has been little progress since 1960.[5]

TABLE 2.—*Average indexes of residential segregation of the white and nonwhite population, for 109 cities, 1940 to 1960*

Year	Total	North and West	South
1940	85.2	85.5	84.9
1950	87.3	86.3	88.5
1960	86.1	82.8	90.7

SOURCE: Karl E. Taeuber and Alma F. Taeuber, *Negroes in Cities*, Chicago, Aldine Publishing Co., 1965, table 5, page 44.

The different income levels of whites and Negroes contribute to the segregated pattern in housing. But race is a far better predictor of where a person will live than is income—or any other attribute. For example, a disproportionate number of Negroes with incomes high enough to afford to live in more prosperous neighborhoods nonetheless live in poverty areas. In 1960 only 12 percent of whites with incomes above the poverty level were living in poverty areas, but two-thirds of all Negroes who had incomes above the poverty line lived in poverty areas. The tendency for Negroes with middle-level incomes to be confined to poverty areas may also help explain the fact, noted in the chapter on "Social Mobility," that middle class Negroes are less likely to be able to pass their status on to their sons than middle class whites.

Racial segregation in housing not only has "social" costs of the sort just described, but also operates as a barrier in the housing market which sometimes denies Negroes their share of the benefits from the increase in the Nation's housing supply. The extent and rigidity of racial segregation in housing suggest that Negroes cannot move into white residential areas without considerable difficulty. To the extent

---

[5] Reynolds Farley and Karl E. Taeuber, "Population Trends and Residential Segregation Since 1960," *Science* (March, 1969), p. 955.

this is true, they are denied access to most of the Nation's housing supply. This in turn would imply that Negroes would have to pay higher rents for comparable housing than whites.

There is evidence that this is often the case. As table 3 shows, in three of the places studied, rents are much higher in mainly Negro neighborhoods than in mainly white neighborhoods with the same percentage of "sound" housing (housing with adequate plumbing, and neither deteriorating nor dilapidated) and the same number of rooms per dwelling. In four other cities, there was probably no meaningful difference in the rent for housing of comparable quality.

TABLE 3.—*Rents paid by Negroes and whites for comparable housing*

City	Average monthly rent in median Negro census tract	Average monthly rent in white census tract with comparable housing	Negro rent minus white rent for comparable housing
Atlanta	$37	$38	−1
Baltimore	66	55	11
Detroit	61	60	1
Los Angeles	58	56	2
New York:			
Manhattan	59	61	−2
Brooklyn	60	51	9
Philadelphia	49	40	9

NOTE.—This estimate was provided by Professor Barbara Bergmann of the Department of Economics at the University of Maryland.

Though the complexity of this problem and the limitations of the data call for caution, these results tend to strengthen the logical presumption that practices which exclude Negroes from most of the housing supply will mean that the pressure of increasing demand by Negroes will force up the prices of the housing they are allowed to occupy. The barrier of residential segregation is particularly important when the Nation's housing supply grows faster than the population: it limits the process by which new housing for the well-to-do can open up better housing for the poor. Since this process is the main source of better housing for the poor, segregation, along with credit, zoning, and other barriers which limit the access of the poor to available housing, are outstandingly important.

City Space and Urban Amenities

Most Americans now live in cities or suburbs. Thus the manmade physical environment includes not only the house or apartment, but also that complex of structures, streets, and services we call the city— or the metropolitan area. The geography of the city, and the transportation system that lets the resident move within it or escape outside it, are therefore important parts of our physical environment.

The metropolitan environment is infinitely varied. But there is a common problem that links the lives of all the residents of a metropolitan area. This problem is the scarcity of urban space, for which all the residents of a metropolis compete, whether they are buying homes or looking for a place to park.

a. POPULATION AND URBAN SPACE

As we argued earlier, Malthus' dismal prediction that population tends to grow faster than food production has lost its credibility, at least for the economically developed nations. But population growth in the United States is posing new kinds of problems, different from those that were expected. One of these is the scarcity of urban space. The growth and increasing concentration of our population deny us privacy and elbow room. Our increasingly congested cities are already depriving many people of the satisfaction of open space. As cities continue to grow, it will be even more difficult to find a quiet park, an open space, or a secluded beach. This problem may already be serious in such areas as Harlem, which has a sardine-can density of 67,000 persons per square mile.

It is not possible to say for certain whether such crowding degrades the quality of life significantly for very many people. Perhaps only a minority want privacy or open space, or can experience claustrophobia. It is evident from any number of parks and beaches that, just as a few seek secluded spots, so many others congregate wherever the most people are.

Animal experiments have shown, however, that severe congestion tends to increase aggressive behavior, to break down normal mating, nesting, and maternal activity, and to contribute to higher rates of illness and death. There may also be a limit to the congestion that human beings can tolerate.

The number of persons that can be accommodated per square mile without serious crowding depends in part on what might be called the "technology" of urban space. It is possible to build more living space on each acre, by building up rather than out, providing communal landscaping and recreational space, using underground transportation, and the like. There are undoubtedly limitations to the number of people who can live satisfactorily in each square mile—the amount of open space with access to sunlight is inherently limited—but a great deal can be done, through imaginative city planning, to make a congested environment congenial.

b. URBAN TRANSPORTATION AND SPACE

The scarcity of urban space can also be eased by more extensive use of transportation. The people of a metropolis can have more space simply by traveling farther out, and that is what many Americans have been doing. They have "traded off" the time and money spent in commuting for the open space available in the suburbs. The move to suburban, single family homes on separate lots suggests that many Americans value space and privacy very highly. There are also, of course, other factors that draw many people to the suburbs. This move has to some extent been subsidized by public policy, encouraged by the desire for better schools, and even hurried at times by prejudice against the groups in the central city.

There is an important, if implicit, subsidy for the move to the suburbs in the tax advantages given homeowners. Homeownership is most common where single family dwellings are common, as in the suburbs, and homeowners pay no income tax on the imputed rent (the extra money they would have had to earn and pay in rent to have the same standard of living with an equivalent rented dwelling) on an owner-occupied dwelling. Homeownership is also subsidized through FHA loans and government loans to veterans. Subsidies to rapid transit systems, though not usually so regarded, sometimes also subsidize the flight to the suburbs. The fact that the central city government must provide services to those who work in the city, yet cannot tax their property in the suburbs, has a similar effect.

The patterns of segregation, and even some zoning laws, suggest that a desire to exclude low income and low status groups also accounts for some movement to the suburbs. This exclusion also creates a further monetary incentive for emigration to the suburbs, since the central city must assume the burden of dealing with poverty and other social problems. The suburbanite often enjoys both better schooling for his children and lower taxes as well.

The desire for space and privacy, along with the inducements to suburbanization, have led to "urban sprawl." Metropolitan areas will tend to expand to the point where they grow together. The vision of one sprawling megalopolis, reaching from Boston to Washington, comes closer to reality each year.

The collision of metropolitan areas shows the undeniable reality of the problem of urban space. But even then the cities can grow in other directions. If the technology of commuter transportation can be made to improve fast enough, and the quality of city planning and land use can be increased fast enough, the sprawling metropolis can still provide a wholesome environment for man.

Chapter IV

Income and Poverty

ARE WE BETTER OFF?

INCOME is a rough but convenient measure of the goods and services—food, clothing, entertainment, medical care, and so forth—available to a person or a family or a nation. This chapter first discusses the general level of income in the United States: What is happening to total and average income for the country as a whole? Next, it describes the distribution of that income: Are incomes becoming more or less equally distributed and how are Negroes faring relative to whites? Third, it discusses poverty: How many people have incomes which are lower than what is generally considered a minimum standard of decency? Finally, this chapter discusses, at somewhat greater length than other chapters, the policy implications of present trends: What are we doing to eliminate poverty and what could we do?

Obviously, income is not the only measure of the well-being of individuals, families, or nations. If two people have the same income but one is sick and one is healthy, the healthy person is clearly better off. Similarly, the well-being of a nation is measured, not just by its level of income, but also by its health, its education, and many other aspects of national life, some of which are discussed in other chapters of this report.

Moreover, people, individually and collectively, often trade income for leisure. As productivity has increased in the United States and other advanced countries, the workweek has fallen. We have chosen to give up additional income for increased leisure.

Money income, of course, cannot buy happiness, and it is by no means obvious that satisfaction rises along with income. Perhaps the very poor in contemporary America feel most dissatisfied with their level of income; perhaps not. It may be those who are most dissatisfied have incomes just below the average and see all about them evidence of a generally high standard of living to which they aspire but cannot reach. Since we cannot measure satisfaction and dissatisfaction, however, we must turn to the more easily measurable statistics of money income.

AFFLUENT AMERICA

The most obvious fact about American income is that it is the highest in the world and rising rapidly. In terms of gross national product per capita—or any other measure of the average availability of goods and services—the United States far outranks its nearest competitors, Canada and the countries of northern Europe. Average incomes in the United States are several orders of magnitude larger than those in the underdeveloped world. (See figure IV–1.)

Aggregate personal income (the amounts paid to individuals in wages, grants, interest, dividends, and other forms) increased from $14 billion at the turn of the century to about $584 billion in 1966 or more than 40-fold. After adjusting for price level increases and population increases, it is estimated that personal income per capita in constant dollars was four times greater in 1966 than at the turn of the century. In other words, those of us living today have four times as much in the way of goods and services as did those living in 1900.

The signs of affluence are everywhere. Americans own more than 60 million automobiles; 95 percent of American households own at least one television set, 25 percent own at least two; and over 60 percent of American families own their own homes.

THE DISTRIBUTION OF INCOME

Although overall income levels are high and rising, the distribution of income in the United States has remained practically unchanged in the last 20 years. As table 1 shows, the Depression of the 1930's brought a sharp drop in the share of the top 5 percent of all families and unrelated individuals and a rise in the share of the lowest 20 percent. World War II brought an even more marked rise in the share of the lowest 20 percent. However, since the mid-1940's, there has been little observable change in the overall distribution of income. The lowest 20 percent of households have consistently received 5 percent or less of personal income and less than 4 percent of total money income.

Perhaps one of the most interesting questions with respect to income and its distribution is what has happened to nonwhites relative to whites.

Income Levels of Whites and Nonwhites: The ratio of nonwhite to white median incomes for several different groups in selected years is shown in table 2. In 1947, the median money income of nonwhite males was a little over half that of white males. By 1966, both groups had money incomes about two-thirds larger ($2,961 and $5,364), but the level for nonwhite men was still only a little over half that of white men. However, the trends for nonwhite women and for nonwhite families as units have been more favorable.

The most dramatic shift has been in the position of nonwhite women. In 1953, the median income of nonwhite women was about 60 percent that of white women. In the North, it was about 80 percent, and in the South it was less than 50 percent. At the end of 1966, the median income of nonwhite women was about 75 percent that of white women. It was above that of white women in all regions except the South where it was slightly more than half that of white women.

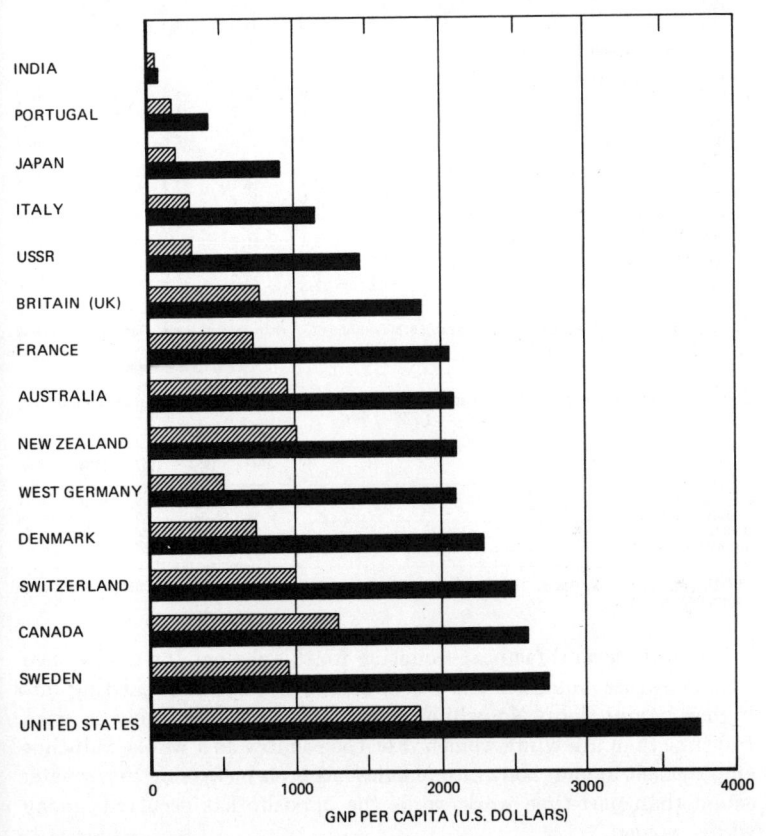

Figure IV-1: Gross National Product Per Capita (1955 and 1966).

[Bar chart showing GNP per capita in U.S. Dollars for 1955 and 1966 for the following countries: INDIA, PORTUGAL, JAPAN, ITALY, USSR, BRITAIN (UK), FRANCE, AUSTRALIA, NEW ZEALAND, WEST GERMANY, DENMARK, SWITZERLAND, CANADA, SWEDEN, UNITED STATES.]

GNP per capita — 1955
Source: Paul Studenski, *The Income of Nations;* New York University Press, 1958; Table 16-3, pp. 229-230.

GNP per capita — 1966
Source: *Statistical Abstract of the U.S.,* 1968 edition, Table 1257, p. 844.

TABLE 1.—*Distribution of personal and money income: mean income and share of aggregate received by each fifth and top 5 percent of families and unrelated individuals, selected years, 1929–1966*

Year and income	Mean income before tax (current dollars)	Lowest fifth	Second fifth	Middle fifth	Fourth fifth	Highest fifth	Top 5 percent
PERSONAL INCOME							
Families and unrelated individuals							
1929	$2,335	12.5		13.8	19.3	54.4	30.0
1935–36	1,631	4.1	9.2	14.1	20.9	51.7	26.5
1944	3,614	4.9	10.9	16.2	22.2	45.8	20.7
1947	4,126	5.0	11.0	16.0	22.0	46.0	20.9
1957	6,238	4.7	11.1	16.3	22.4	45.5	20.2
1962	7,262	4.6	10.9	16.3	22.7	45.5	19.6
MONEY INCOME							
Families and unrelated individuals							
1947	3,224	3.5	10.5	16.7	23.5	45.8	19.0
1957	4,861	3.4	10.8	17.9	24.8	43.1	16.7
1962	6,049	3.5	10.3	17.3	24.5	44.3	17.3
1966	7,425	3.7	10.5	17.4	24.6	43.8	16.8
Families							
1947	3,566	5.1	11.8	16.7	23.2	43.3	17.5
1957	5,483	5.0	12.6	18.1	23.7	40.5	15.8
1962	6,811	5.1	12.0	17.3	23.8	41.7	16.3
1966	8,423	5.4	12.3	17.7	23.7	41.0	15.3
Unrelated individuals							
1947	1,692	2.9	5.4	11.5	21.3	58.9	33.3
1957	2,253	2.9	7.2	13.6	25.3	51.0	19.7
1962	2,800	3.3	7.3	12.5	24.1	52.8	21.3
1966	3,490	2.8	7.5	13.2	23.8	52.7	22.5

SOURCE: Ida C. Merriam, "Welfare and its Measurement," *Indicators of Social Change*, Sheldon & Moore, eds., p. 735.

TABLE 2.—*Ratio of nonwhite to white median incomes for selected groups and years, 1947–1966*

	1947	1953	1957	1964	1966
Males 14 and over	0.54	0.55	0.47	0.57	0.55
Females 14 and over	.49	.59	.62	.70	.76
Families	.51	.56	.54	.56	.60
Unrelated individuals	.72	.80	.67	.69	.73

SOURCE: Ida C. Merriam, "Welfare and its Measurement," *Indicators of Social Change*, Sheldon & Moore, eds., p. 744.

There are several factors accounting for this change. It would appear that nonwhite women in the North and West have been shifting into higher paying jobs. Nonwhite women are also more likely to work full time than are white women. For the country as a whole, full-time employment among nonwhite females has been increasing to a greater extent than part-time work, while the opposite has occurred among white women.

In interpreting these differences, several factors are important. The longer hours worked by nonwhite women have been noted. Nonwhite men, on the other hand, experience more unemployment or part-time employment than do white men. Nonwhites, both men and women, are generally employed in the low-paying occupations. Beyond this, there is some indication that even within the same occupations, there may be significant differentials in the opportunity to advance.

One analysis, which takes account of the effects of family background, education, mental ability, number of siblings, and occupation concludes that perhaps one-third of the difference in average income (for 1961) between Negroes and whites "arises because Negro and white men in the same line of work, with the same amount of formal schooling, with equal ability, from families of the same size and the same socioeconomic level simply do not draw the same wages and salaries."[1]

Measured by income levels, nonwhites have made substantial progress in absolute terms and, to a lesser degree, in comparison to whites. However, the degree of inequality of income among nonwhites has chnaged very little.

Table 3 shows how total nonwhite income was shared by nonwhites. As in the overall distribution of income in the U.S., there has been little change in the share of the lowest 20 percent of nonwhite households. In 1947, the lowest 20 percent received 4.8 percent of total money income. In 1966, their share stood at 4.7 percent. There does, however, seem to be a rising trend in the share of this group beginning with 1960.

TABLE 3.—*Total money income of nonwhite families: mean income and percentage share received by each fifth and top 5 percent, 1947–1966*

Year	Mean income	Lowest fifth	Second fifth	Middle fifth	Fourth fifth	Highest fifth	Top 5 percent
1947	$2,016	4.8	10.2	15.7	23.6	45.8	17.0
1948	2,104	4.3	10.1	16.9	24.4	44.3	16.6
1949	1,965	3.8	9.9	16.6	24.6	45.1	17.1
1950	2,128	3.8	9.7	17.9	25.1	43.4	16.6
1951	2,368	3.8	10.3	16.9	25.3	43.8	16.1
1952	2,639	5.0	11.4	17.9	23.7	41.9	16.0
1953	2,890	3.9	10.7	17.0	25.1	43.4	15.2
1954	2,758	3.6	10.0	17.2	25.8	43.4	15.5
1955	2,890	4.0	10.3	17.8	25.5	42.4	14.3
1956	3,073	3.9	10.5	17.2	25.3	43.1	15.0
1957	3,241	3.6	10.2	16.9	26.0	43.1	15.0
1958	3,351	4.0	9.9	16.2	25.0	44.9	17.0
1959	3,523	4.1	9.5	16.5	25.3	44.7	16.2
1960	3,913	3.9	9.6	16.4	25.4	44.7	16.2
1961	4,031	4.0	9.6	15.9	24.5	46.0	17.4
1962	4,020	4.2	10.6	16.6	24.2	44.5	16.3
1963	4,340	4.4	10.2	16.1	24.6	44.7	17.2
1964	4,772	4.5	10.5	16.2	24.3	44.6	16.7
1965	4,903	4.6	10.7	16.5	24.7	43.5	15.5
1966	5,526	4.7	10.7	16.8	24.9	42.9	15.4

SOURCE: Ida Merriam, "Welfare and its Measurement," *Indicators of Social Change*, Sheldon & Moore, eds., p. 797.

It may also be significant that in 1947 nonwhites comprised 8.3 percent of the families in the lowest 20 percent of all families (whites comprised 91.7 percent), and received 4.1 percent of the total income which accrued to this group of families (whites received 95.9 percent). In 1966, nonwhites accounted for 10 percent of the families in the

---

[1] Otis Dudley Duncan, *Inheritance of Poverty or Inheritance of Race* (forthcoming).

lowest 20 percent of all families and received 5.5 percent of the income.

POVERTY

Although the distribution of income has remained virtually unchanged, rising income levels have meant that fewer and fewer people have incomes below the "poverty line."

In 1963, the Council of Economic Advisers established a tentative level of "poverty income" of $1,500 or less per year for individuals and $3,000 or less per year for families of two or more. By that standard, there were 33 million poor Americans in 1963. The standard was a useful first approximation; but, it obviously was only that.

To gain a greater understanding of the nature and composition of our poor population, the Social Security Administration developed new criteria built around minimum food requirements. The amounts required to purchase necessary food are based on the Department of Agriculture's "economy food plan." This plan is described as "for temporary or emergency use when funds are low." The base established by the food budget is raised by a factor of approximately three to allow for the minimum amounts necessary to purchase housing, clothing, medical care, etc. Adjustments are also made to reflect differences in family size, age, and farm or nonfarm residence. In 1966, the poverty level for a nonaged, nonfarm, male headed family of four was $3,335. Using this standard, the poor numbered some 40 million persons in 1960. By 1967, that number had dropped to 26 million (the most recent year for which poverty statistics are available).

The decline in poverty came during a unique period of sustained economic expansion and in the midst of increased governmental efforts to alleviate the poverty problem. Not surprisingly, the benefits of economic growth and of the War on Poverty have fallen unevenly on the poor population. As table 4 shows, the sharpest declines have been in those families headed by an able-bodied working man. From 1961 to 1966, the number of nonaged, male-headed poor families declined by more than 35 percent. In contrast, the number of aged poor households declined by about 6 percent, and among the unemployed and families headed by a female, the decline was less than 5 percent.

Although the reduction in poverty has been impressive among some groups, an extrapolation of past trends suggests that poverty in the United States is not likely to disappear in the near future even for those groups. With a 4 percent rate of growth in GNP (in constant dollars, which is higher than the average growth since 1960), there are likely to be close to 17 million persons in poor households in 1974 compared to 26

TABLE 4.—*Poor households, 1961–1966, by age, family status, and sex of family head*

Status	1961 number	1966 number	Percent change
Total households (thousands) (excluding military)	12,881	10,826	−16
Nonaged households	8,360	6,591	−21
Families	6,149	4,476	−27
Male headed families	4,579	2,900	−37
White	3,416	2,102	−39
Worked	3,005	1,740	−42
Didn't work	411	362	−13
Nonwhite	1,163	797	−32
Worked	1,060	691	−35
Didn't work	103	106	+2
Female headed families	1,570	1,576	(*)
White	939	934	−1
Worked	451	460	+1
Didn't work	488	474	−3
Nonwhite	631	642	+1
Worked	383	376	−3
Didn't work	248	266	+7
Unrelated individuals	2,211	2,115	−4
Male	815	712	−13
White	567	534	−6
Worked	421	386	−8
Didn't work	146	148	+1
Nonwhite	248	178	−28
Worked	186	116	−38
Didn't work	62	62	0
Female	1,396	1,403	(*)
White	1,048	1,079	+3
Worked	590	571	−3
Didn't work	458	508	+10
Nonwhite	348	324	−7
Worked	204	199	−3
Didn't work	144	125	−13
Aged households	4,521	4,235	−6

*Less than 0.5 percent.

million in 1967. Of these, more than 4 million will be in families headed by a nonaged working male compared to 10 million in 1967. Moreover, unless we are more successful than in the past in dealing with the problem of inadequate income among the aged, and among those in families headed by a female or an unemployed male, these groups will still account for 11 million poor persons in 1974, compared to 13 million in 1967.

Again, it is important to emphasize that these estimates are based on a poverty standard which, by 1974, will have remained unchanged for 15 years except for adjustments to reflect changes in the cost of living. Should our notion of what constitutes a minimum income change during this period, the forecast of poverty made above would be even more bleak.

THE PATTERN OF PRESENT PROGRAMS

The incidence of poverty and the distribution of income are overwhelmingly determined by the operation of the Nation's economic system. In large part, this means earnings for work.

Employment and wages depend primarily on the tastes, preferences and incomes of consumers, the technology used in producing goods, the productivity of labor as determined by education, experience, age, skill levels, and so forth, and the supply of labor. Overlaying these basic forces are other factors which also have a powerful effect on employment and wages. These include the bargaining power of labor unions and discriminatory practices with respect to the aged, women, and nonwhites.

Since the wage system is driven primarily by market forces, it does not necessarily insure everyone an adequate income or an equitable distribution of income for the Nation as a whole.

The programs which have evolved since the 1930's to deal with the shortcomings of the wage system fall essentially into two categories. On the one hand, insurance type solutions have been applied in cases where loss of earnings is due to a severing or weakening of the tie to the labor force due to age, disability, death, or unemployment. This approach has been supplemented by a more or less parallel system of public assistance for those individuals not covered by the insurance type mechanism or for whom protection, though available, is inadequate.

On the other hand, solutions to the problem of low income for those who work have been primarily concerned with increasing the level and coverage of the minimum wage and, more recently, with a series of human investment programs designed to help individuals become more productive members of the labor force. The Federal Government has not directly intervened in the market place to supplement the earnings of those who work but still have inadequate incomes.

Although this section is confined to a discussion of those programs which provide a direct transfer of money income from one group to another or increase the income of some groups relative to others through the wage system, it is important to realize that almost every Government program can and does have an effect on the distribution of real income and wealth (physical and human), sometimes explicitly, sometimes implicitly. Government programs to finance the cost of health services for large segments of our population are examples of a large and explicit redistribution in which the beneficiaries receive a service at a much lower cost (or no cost) rather than money incomes. The Food Stamp Program is another example.

What is not frequently realized is that other Government policies, such as provisions for tax deduction of interest paid on owner-occupied homes, for oil depletion allowances, and for farm price supports represent intentional and unintentional transfers in the other direction.

With these thoughts in mind, we now turn to a discussion of some of the more important programs affecting the distribution of income.

Social Insurance: It is fair to say that our insurance type programs have worked better and gained greater acceptance than either our public assistance programs or those designed to aid the working poor. This is undoubtedly due, in large part, to the idea that protection grows out of the work that people do, with eligibility for, and the amount of, benefits related to past earnings and contributions. Also characteristic is the absence of any individualized means test. Just about all industrial countries now base their "income maintenance" systems on social insurance.

In the United States, the largest and most important of the social insurance programs is the Federal system popularly called social security. This program insures against the loss of earnings due to retirement, disability or death and pays benefits to meet the great bulk of hospital and medical costs in old age.

This year, 90 million people will contribute to social security. Ninety percent of our population age 65 and over are eligible for monthly social security benefits. More than 95 out of 100 young children and their mothers are eligible for monthly benefits in the event the family breadwinner should die. Four out of five people of working age have income protection against loss of earnings due to long-term severe disability of the breadwinner. When the Federal civil service system, the railroad retirement program, and State and local government staff retirement systems are taken into account, nearly everyone now has protection under a Government program against the risk of loss of earned income for selected causes.

Public Assistance: Public assistance and programs for the working poor have worked less well. In 1965, only 20 percent of poor persons received public assistance payments and, of these, 82 percent remained poor after payment. Payment levels are erratic with wide State-by-State differences; in New York, for example, the average monthly payment for a family of four on Aid for Dependent Children is almost $250, compared to $115 in Ohio and $35 in Mississippi. Moreover, the determination of eligibility has frequently been made by procedures which detract from dignity and which stigmatize the recipient as being on relief or the beneficiary of a welfare handout.

The program of Aid to Families with Dependent Children has come in for the lion's share of the criticism of present welfare programs. Originally conceived as a program for widowed mothers and their children, over time, the character of the program has changed; the source of dependency has been rooted less and less in the death or incapacitation of the father and increasingly in socially less acceptable causes—the absence of a father due to divorce, desertion, imprisonment, or even the lack of a legal father.

At the same time, public attitudes toward working mothers have become less negative and in the postwar period, there has been a tremendous upsurge in labor force participation of married women.

Both of these facts must form the backdrop for understanding the recent attacks on public assistance. Not only have payment levels been so miserably low in some places that the perpetuation of poverty from one generation to another seems inevitable, but paradoxically, the program has contributed to the creation of dependency for less socially acceptable causes—family breakups—and at the same time has stultified individual initiative and self-help because of the fact that additional income from earnings or elsewhere meant an equal reduction in assistance payments, in effect a 100 percent tax rate on earnings.

Recently enacted changes in public assistance should improve the program on the latter point. After July 1, 1969, recipients of AFDC will be permitted to exempt the first $30 of earnings and one-third of earnings above that in determining assistance levels. In addition, the 1967 Amendments established a Work Incentive Program of training and education, and increased support for day care and related services to enhance the employability of AFDC recipients.

Minimum Wage and Training Programs: Minimum wage legislation, as a solution for the problem of the working poor, has been criticized by its supporters for establishing a minimum wage level which is too low and for restricting coverage too narrowly. It has been attacked by its critics on the grounds that it results in significant unemployment of marginal workers and that this loss outweighs the gain in higher wages for those who remain employed. Hard data on the quantitative effects are lacking.

Advocates and skeptics also abound with respect to manpower training programs, and in some sense over the same issues: coverage and effectiveness.

Although no analyses are available which resolve these issues, it is clear that even if there were no employment effects, increases in the minimum wage would be an inefficient and not totally effective way of redistributing income because:

—It does not distinguish between large and small families. Adequate levels for small families would be inadequate for large ones.

—Many households have inadequate incomes, but no connection with the labor force.

—Many of the poor work intermittently. A high minimum wage would not assure them adequate annual incomes.

It is also clear that, even under the most optimistic assumptions about the effectiveness of manpower training programs, these programs alone cannot be an entirely satisfactory solution to the problems of income redistribution because:

—It would take 5 to 10 years to reach all of the employable poor even with much heavier funding than at present.

—We have few programs that deal with persons at the lower end of the income distribution who work full time (or even part time).

In 1966, about one-third of the persons in poverty were in families headed by a man or woman who worked all year.

Finally, it should be noted that there are some ethical issues involved. Even if everybody who was employable had training and/or a job there would be a good deal of variance in income levels. Wages are largely a function of skill levels. The skill levels with which one enters the labor force are largely a function of the opportunities available in early life to get education, training, and to grow up healthy. Yet, the opportunity structure is not uniformly open.

This has meant that the risk of poverty is much greater for some than others, and that for these the poverty of one generation is more likely to be perpetuated in the next. Children born into poor families will not only be poor children, but face a higher probability that they will be poor adults and that they, themselves, will raise poor children. There is mounting evidence that malnutrition in early childhood may cause permanent and irremediable mental retardation. Children in poor families often tend to drop out of school to contribute to the family support, an action that drastically increases the risk of being poor adults. It is unrealistic to suppose that training programs can overcome all the barriers to obtaining an adequate income exclusively from the wage system when these same barriers are the product of an imperfect opportunity structure.

However, even if we had a completely equal opportunity structure, there would still be a question of equity. Under these circumstances, the distribution of income from earnings would largely reflect distributions among the general population of abilities that are in demand in the labor market—primarily intelligence. It is quite conceivable that the resulting income distribution would still be unsatisfactory on social grounds and one could argue for systematic redistribution of income.

The next section looks at some of the alternatives which are currently being considered for achieving such a redistribution.

INCOME MAINTENANCE ALTERNATIVES

Without question, there is a growing consensus that social security programs need improvement, that public assistance is badly in need of reform, and that better ways must be found to help the working poor and their families. There is no lack of statements on the subject of income maintenance by business and labor groups, Government officials, those from the academic community, and the press. The question, it seems, is not whether, but how, and on that, there is far from a consensus.

The issue of "how" revolves around two fundamental but interrelated questions:

—To what extent can present programs be modified to develop a more adequate system of economic security?

—Which of the major new proposals put forward in recent years should be selected to round out the Nation's system of income maintenance?

With respect to social security, the specific issues raised by the first question concern the benefit structure, the benefit levels, program coverage, and the financing of benefits. Social security is a social insurance program. As is the case in most countries with such programs, the benefits replace a higher proportion of previous earnings for low than for high income groups and minimum benefit levels have been established. A small number of aged persons have been blanketed into the program with benefits financed from general revenues. Benefit levels have been adjusted from time to time to reflect rising price and real income levels. To what extent should social security be further modified to provide additional income to the poor?

As a practical matter, the answer probably depends on how successful we can be in reforming our present welfare system or developing a new program based on need. To the extent that a decent standard of living for the aged, the disabled, and surviving widows and children can be insured through a humanely administered program of public welfare or a negative income tax, it can be argued that to try to refashion social security so that it meets all income maintenance needs would be inefficient, and possibly detrimental to the program.

The question of how and whether public assistance should be modified is a complex one. One proposal which has been put forward would federalize the system for the present federally aided categories, establish minimum standards at the poverty level, and finance the program entirely with Federal funds.

Such a program would overcome many of the defects of the present system:

—Within categories, much of the wide variation in payment levels in present programs would be eliminated.

—The program would be more adequate in terms of coverage—by 1974, between 70 and 75 percent of those who are poor would fall in the categories eligible for aid and would receive it compared to 55 percent under present programs.

—The programs would be more adequate in terms of level of support—by 1974, it would close about 60 percent of the total poverty gap.

—The program would provide substantial financial relief for the States by removing the shared cost of the present Federal/State public assistance program. By 1974, the States would realize a saving of about $4 billion in welfare costs which could be allocated to other uses.

Despite these improvements, however, the program has several distinct drawbacks:

—The poor in households headed by a male who works, numbering about 10 million in 1967, and expected to account for about 5 million persons in 1974, would not be eligible for supplementation.

—The program would provide a substantial monetary incentive for the adult members of intact families to establish separate households.

—The program would intensify already serious equity problems with respect to different treatment of poor families headed by a male who works and those headed by a female who works. A man with a wife and two children who works full time would receive no supplementation whereas a woman with three children who works full time and earns the same amount could receive a substantial amount of additional support. This difference is much less under present programs because of the low payment levels in some States for female headed families.

As these facts suggest, the problem of income inadequacy cannot be completely solved by reforms in public assistance. The third major building block in addition to social security improvements and welfare reform should be designed to close the remaining gaps in our income maintenance system. The main options which have been advanced are the Negative Income Tax and Children's Allowance.

The negative income tax would provide income supplementation to everyone on the basis of an income test. The allowance would be reduced fractionally as other income, particularly earnings, increased. Because the negative income tax program is income tested, and comprehensive in coverage, it is an effective and efficient tool for achieving whatever degree of income redistribution is desired.

The children's allowance is a "demogrant" program; that is, entitlement is based on a demographic characteristic, in this case, age. Benefits would be paid to all families based on the number and perhaps the age of the children. It would not, of course, meet the income needs of other groups, and thus would have to be part of a multiprogram package including public assistance, social security, and so on.

The chief advantage of the children's allowance is that it is not income tested. It is also its chief disadvantage. Programs without an income test do not develop the stigma associated with programs that have an income test. Being on social security is not demeaning. Being on public assistance can be and frequently is. The basic argument in favor of using an income test is that it more efficiently channels funds to those who are needy. Transferring funds on the basis of age or sex, rather than on the basis of need, means that many nonneedy persons are eligible and thus the percentage of total benefits going to the poor may be small.

It is precisely this inefficiency which has led most children's allowance proponents to include "recoupment" features in their plans. One common recoupment plan would eliminate the $600 children's exemption in the present tax laws. This, and similar plans, tend to move the costs of children's allowance programs toward a negative income tax for children.

In summary, there is no such thing as a single, simple answer to the problems of poverty and of economic security. There are no magic solutions. We will unquestionably continue our multifaceted attack on the problem.

Nearly 35 years ago, in a message to Congress preceding the passage of the Social Security Act, President Roosevelt outlined the goal that still lies before us:

Our task of reconstruction does not require the creation of new and strange values. It is rather the finding of the way once more to known, but to some degree forgotten, ideals and values. If the means and details are in some instances new, the objectives are as permanent as human nature.

Among our objectives I place the security of the men, women, and children of the Nation first.

This security for the individual and for the family concerns itself primarily with three factors. People want decent homes to live in; they want to locate them where they can engage in productive work; and they want some safeguard against misfortunes which cannot be wholly eliminated in this manmade world of ours.

Chapter V

Public Order and Safety

WHAT IS THE IMPACT OF CRIME ON OUR LIVES?

TO ASSESS THE QUALITY OF AMERICAN LIFE, we must consider the impact of crime on our society. People neither want to be the victims of crime nor to live in fear of crime. Moreover, crime challenges the basic assumptions of civilized society. A society cannot claim to be minimally civilized if greed and aggression are regularly permitted to override respect for other people.

An increase in crime has a variety of implications for the well being of a society. It is reflected in the workload of the police, the amount of harm to victims, and the prevalence of criminal behavior and attitudes. The impact of crime needs to be appraised from each of these perspectives to determine how crime can best be prevented and controlled.

For these purposes it is best to concentrate on crimes generally considered most serious. There is a set of actions which almost every society has felt it necessary to combat. These include criminal homicide, assault, rape, and different varieties of theft. Because such actions have been prohibited at almost all times and places by a nearly universal consent, the study of these crimes answers best to the needs of social reporting for data, for meaningful comparisons, and for phenomena of clear concern to our society.[1]

INCREASES IN MAJOR CRIMES

The periodic reports of law enforcement agencies to the Federal Bureau of Investigation show large and persistent increases in the numbers of known crimes. The FBI statistics show increases in major crimes generally considered serious of 13 percent in 1964, 6 percent in

---

[1] It should not be forgotten, however, that other sorts of crimes create an immense caseload for the police and the courts. Over half of all arrests are for public drunkenness, drunk driving, other liquor offenses, disorderly conduct, vagrancy, and gambling.

1965, 11 percent in 1966, and 17 percent in 1967.[2] Major crimes have been increasing faster than the population. The FBI index of major crimes per hundred thousand population increased at an average rate of 8.7 percent per year between 1958 and 1967.

Different types of crime have been increasing at very different rates. Indeed, the homicide rate was actually lower in 1967 than in 1933. From 1958 to 1967 FBI index crimes per 100,000 population increased at the following average annual rates:

Homicide	— 2.9%
Rape	— 5.6%
Aggravated assault	— 7.8%
Robbery	— 10.0%
Burglary	— 8.4%
Larceny	— 9.9%
Auto theft	— 8.2%

The Problem of Underreporting

It has long been known that there has been a difference between the total number of crimes and those officially reported. In fact, sample surveys undertaken for the President's Crime Commission in 1965 indicate that *several* times as many crimes occur as are reported in official crime statistics. One explanation is that the victims of crime often do not report incidents because of the circumstances in which a crime occurs. Assaults, for example, commonly occur among members of the same family or among neighbors and the participants involved often prefer to make their own peace with each other. If a juvenile steals something it may seem kinder to obtain restitution through his parents rather than through the police.

THE HARM DONE TO VICTIMS

In addition to information on the number of significant criminal offenses, we need to know how much harm these offenses do to their victims. If in a given year there were 90 more murders and 100 fewer burglaries, most people would surely say that victims had suffered more, though the number of criminal offenses would be less. We need a way of "weighting" each crime that occurs according to the amount of harm it does.

So that a burglary will not count as much as a murder, property crimes could be weighted by the average amount of the dollar loss

---

[2] The FBI Index of Crime is composed of murder and willful manslaughter, forcible rape, robbery (involving at least the threat of personal violence in an attempt to steal), aggravated assault, burglary (with or without the use of force), larceny (stealing without the use of force or fraud), and automobile theft. Arson and kidnaping are the most obviously serious crimes *not* included.

which results and murders weighted by some appropriately much greater figure. A very conservative, if not callous, figure would be the projected life-time earnings of an individual, perhaps $200,000. This weighting procedure would be crude, but it would be far less misleading than counting every crime equally as one. To illustrate, there were on average 298,661 burglaries reported in the years 1938 to 1942. There were on average 7,525 murders in the same years. In a later 5-year period, 1952 to 1956, there were an average of 491,864 burglaries and 7,000 murders. The total number of the two crimes per year was 192,678 greater on average in the second period. But if we weight the burglaries in constant dollars and the murders by $200,000, even this crude and illustrative weighting would strongly suggest that there was less harm to victims.

Vulnerability and Property Risks

Information on the aggregate amount of harm resulting from crime would tell us something important from the victims' point of view, but not enough. Different people—or the same people at different times—are vulnerable in different degrees. A physical injury which represents a brief period of pain and inconvenience to a young person can be catastropic to an older one. A loss of a few dollars might hardly be missed by a rich man, but felt sorely by a poor one.

Analogously, we need to ask questions about the vulnerability of whole societies or the same society at different times. How much does crime hurt the members of a society, given their ages, activities, wealth and way of life?

If we cansider only crimes of theft against property we can estimate both the amount of harm and the degree of our vulnerability. We can estimate the dollar losses from such crimes from FBI statistics going as far back as the thirties. At the same time, we can contrive a very crude dollar measure of our vulnerability over the same period. We can estimate the dollar value of consumer durables in each year together with the amount of currency in circulation in that year as the measure of our wealth exposed to theft. This makes it possible to say whether the rapacity of criminals is gaining on the growing wealth of the country, or lagging behind it.

Has a dollar in property values become safer or less safe from the common forms of theft? Table 1 shows that by the above calculation the overall risk per $1,000 has increased from $3.55 to $3.91 from 1938 through 1967. For robbery, larceny, and auto theft it was less than in 1938 as recently as 1965; but for burglary it was already considerably greater.

TABLE 1.—*Value of property involved in theft (whether recovered or not) per $1,000 of appropriable property* [1]

Year	Robbery	Burglary	Larceny	Auto theft	Total loss
1967	0.14	1.18	0.79	1.80	3.91
1966	.12	.99	.73	1.65	3.48
1965	.11	.94	.68	1.57	3.30
1964	.12	.89	*.71	1.63	*3.35
1963	.11	.80	.67	1.33	2.90
1962	.09	.70	.58	1.18	2.55
1961	.11	.68	.56	1.08	2.43
1960	*.11	*.66	*.54	*1.09	*2.41
1959	.07	.54	.47	1.00	2.08
1958	.07	.55	*.46	.99	*2.08
1957	.06	.45	.53	1.12	2.16
1956	.06	.43	.51	1.09	2.09
1955	.07	.43	.48	1.02	2.00
1954	.08	.50	.54	1.13	2.24
1953	.08	.45	.55	1.35	2.43
1952	.08	.50	.61	1.43	2.63
1951	.07	.39	.47	1.30	2.23
1950	.10	.40	.46	1.16	2.12
1949	.09	.42	.51	1.20	2.22
1948	.11	.48	.62	1.48	2.69
1947	.12	.55	.67	1.60	2.94
1946	.13	.63	.74	1.94	3.44
1945	.12	.57	.70	2.19	3.58
1944	.08	.45	.60	1.90	3.02
1943	.07	.37	.56	1.66	2.66
1942	.08	.36	.56	1.52	2.52
1941	.13	.42	.62	1.90	3.07
1940	.13	.42	.57	1.83	2.95
1939	.15	.47	.62	1.90	3.14
1938	.15	.52	.69	2.20	3.55

[1] Appropriable property respresents currency in circulation plus a rough estimate of the stock of consumer durable goods.
*Data not strictly comparable to previous year.

The Uneven Burden

There are groups in our society which bear a larger share of the harm done by crime than others. Those most likely to be victims of major crimes—poor Negroes living in the central city—appear to have a rate of victimization several times that of those least likely to be victims—middle-income whites living in a suburb or rural area (see tables 2 and 3).

In general, victimization rates tend to decline as one moves outward from central cities to rural areas. This tendency is pronounced for violent crimes against the person, which seem to show a central city rate five times greater than that of small cities and rural areas. Property crimes, on the other hand, show a rate only twice as great. The rates of "white collar crimes" such as forgery, counterfeiting, and the various types of fraud do not seem to vary with the type of community.

The Response to Risk

How do different groups in the population respond to their different risks? Many people are seriously frightened by the risk of crime, and forego certain activties in order to minimize this risk, such as working or seeking entertainment in certain areas of cities where they live. It would be valuable to know the extent of such dislocations, for they detract significantly from the quality of life.

TABLE 2.—*Victimization by age and sex*

(Rates per 100,000 population)

Offense	Male						
	10–19	20–29	30–39	40–49	50–59	60 plus	All ages
Total	951	5,924	6,231	5,150	4,231	3,465	3,091
Robbery	61	257	112	210	181	98	112
Aggravated assault	399	824	337	263	181	146	287
Burglary	123	2,782	3,649	2,365	2,297	2,343	1,583
Larceny ($50+)	337	1,546	1,628	1,839	967	683	841
Auto theft	31	515	505	473	605	195	268

	Female						
	10–19	20–29	30–39	40–49	50–59	60 plus	All ages
Total	334	2,424	1,514	1,908	1,132	1,052	1,059
Forcible rape	91	238	104	48	0	0	83
Robbery	0	238	157	96	60	81	77
Aggravated assault	91	333	52	286	119	40	118
Burglary	30	665	574	524	298	445	314
Larceny ($50+)	122	570	470	620	536	405	337
Auto theft	0	380	157	334	119	81	130

SOURCE: 1965 Survey by the National Opinion Research Center for the President's Commission on Law Enforcement and Administration of Justice.

TABLE 3.—*Victimization by race and income*

(Rates per 100,000 population)*

Offenses	White			
	$0–$2,999	$3,000–$5,999	$6,000–$9,999	Above $10,000
Total	2,124	2,267	1,685	2,170
Homicide	0	0	0	0
Forcible rape	58	46	0	17
Robbery	116	91	42	34
Aggravated assault	146	289	147	220
Burglary	1,310	958	764	763
Larceny ($50+)	378	700	565	916
Auto theft	116	183	167	220

	Nonwhite		
	$0–$2,999	$3,000–$5,999	$6,000+
Total	2,894	2,581	3,387
Homicide	56	0	0
Forcible rape	111	60	121
Robbery	278	240	121
Aggravated assault	389	420	121
Burglary	1,336	1,261	2,056
Larceny ($50+)	501	300	363
Auto theft	223	300	605

*Rate per 100,000 population of each specific race and income group.

SOURCE: 1965 Survey by the National Opinion Research Center for the President's Commission on Law Enforcement and Administration of Justice.

Information on the character of such dislocations was obtained by the President's Crime Commission. Sixteen percent of respondents in one survey said they had recently wanted to go out but had stayed home because of fear for their own safety. One out of three Negroes had done so and one out of eight whites. Those who were worried about burglary and robbery were 50 percent more likely to take precautions (such as installing locks or bars on windows and keeping firearms) than those who were not.

The Commission also discovered, however, that there was no clear relationship between having been a victim or witness of crime and the taking of precautions. There was a similar lack of clear relationship between the relative rate of crime in a respondent's neighborhood and his perception of it.

THE DEGREE OF CRIMINALITY IN AMERICAN SOCIETY

The harm criminals do to their victims is the main reason we are concerned about crime, but it is not the only reason. The crimes that are committed call in question the decency of our society and the dependability of our social institutions.

When assessing the criminality or law abidingness of a population it is necessary to consider the age distribution of the population. Since young people commit a disproportionate share of crime at all times, it would be possible for the crime rate to increase with a growing proportion of young people even if the propensities of *both* older and younger age groups remained the same.

This possibility is pointed up by the fact that for any one-year age bracket, the greatest number of people arrested for rape, aggravated assault and robbery are age 18, for burglary probably age 15, for auto theft age 16. Crime rates for all age cohorts fall off as their members get older, the rates for the lesser property crimes as early as age 16 or 17, the rates for the major crimes considerably later.

Part of the recent increase in crime rates can thus be attributed to the growing proportion of young people in the population, since there were more adolescents and young adults in the United States in the sixties, relative to the rest of the population, than there were in the fifties. But part of the increase apparently must also be attributed to greater criminality among the young. The percentage increase in juvenile arrest rates from 1960 to 1967 was nearly a third more than that for adults. Arrest rates themselves may not be a good indicator, but they point to the possibility that the propensity of youth to crime is increasing.

If we take into account the size and age composition of the population, the rate of increase in criminality over the past decade appears to have been less than the rate of increase in the absolute number of reported crimes. In 1958, there were 1,573,210 major crimes officially reported; in 1967, there were 3,802,300 such crimes, an increase of 142 percent, for a compound annual rate of increase of 10.3 percent. The rate of such crimes per 100,000 population was 903.6 in 1958 and 1,921.7 in 1967. This crime rate increased 113 percent, for an annual rate of 8.7 percent. But if the proportion of young people, ages 13 to 20, had been the same in 1967 as in 1958, there would have been fewer crimes, a 92 percent increase in the rate, for an annual rate of increase of 7.5 percent.

CRIME PREVENTION

If "crime does not pay," it is because society tries hard to see that it does not. It hires policemen and prosecutors and punishes those convicted of crime.

It is natural that any increase in crime or fear of crime should bring forth demands to apprehend more criminals and punish them more severely. Just as higher wages should attract more labor, so harsher punishments and greater probabilities of apprehension and conviction should deter more crime.

Incentives That Deter Crime

There is obviously much to be said for this "deterrence" or incentive-oriented approach to the crime problem. Fear of punishment undoubtedly deters some crime. Moreover, if the legal system can, in fact, succeed in inflicting harm only on the guilty, this approach appeals to the sense of justice, in a way that police harrassment of "suspicious characters" or preventive detention do not. And unlike vengeance, it has a positive social purpose.

The implications of this approach are, however, a good deal less clearcut than they seem to be. If the theory is not properly stated and qualified it can be a disastrous guide to policy. The conclusion that an increased concern about crime demands harsher punishments is in need of distinction and qualification.

One alternative to harsher punishment is greater reward for legitimate and socially useful activity. For example, there is not much doubt that the poor have higher crime rates for the major and violent crimes than those who are well off. That there is a relationship between poverty and crime is clear, although its precise nature is not.

It is most unlikely that the greater involvement of the poor in criminal activities can be explained entirely, if at all, in terms of the relative severity of potential punishment. In law the punishment is not supposed to vary with the income of the criminal. The social and economic loss resulting from a criminal record are probably greater for those who are well off, but on the other hand, it has been observed that the well-off often receive milder sentences. The rewards for legitimate activity are, on the other hand, systematically and considerably greater for the well-off than for the poor, and this makes crime a relatively less attractive alternative for them than for the poor. Thus informal penalties and incentives to lawful and productive activity seem more likely to explain the difference between the crime rates of rich and poor than the formal deterrents of the law. Adding plausibility to this view is the fact that those with a criminal record are more likely to commit further crimes and have fewer opportunities for legitimate activity because of their criminal records.

The Complexity of Criminal Motivation

Whether a potential criminal is tempted to commit a criminal act or not depends on his perception of the alternatives open to him. There is always a risk that the criminal may be caught, and the potential criminal may perceive such a risk. But he is not likely to be deterred from committing a criminal act by the perception that there is a small chance that he will be severely punished.

The fact that the criminal is often confident he will not be caught, and may be disposed to taking chances, does not mean that harsher punishments would not deter some crime. But if punishments are already sufficiently severe that few will commit criminal acts unless they are disposed to take chances and think the odds are good that they will not be caught, then somewhat more severe punishments can often have only a minor deterrent effect.

This line of reasoning does, however, argue that additions to police forces that are large enough to make it clear to everyone that he is very likely to get caught if he commits a crime would have a significant deterrent effect. And there is clear evidence that more intensive police deployment does, in fact, have such effects. When authorities saturate a high crime area with policemen, the crime rate in the area drops dramatically.

Most crimes are committed by the young, whose experience and knowledge are limited. The alternatives a young person considers, and his evaluation of them, depend particularly on what he learns from his family and friends. Presumably most children brought up in fortunate circumstances never even consider becoming criminals. They know crime is wrong, realize it doesn't pay, and are intellectually and emotionally prepared for legitimate careers. They are, moreover, taught to look upon the police and the system of law and order as something that helps and protects them.

For some young Americans, the situation is very different. They grow up in miserable circumstances and are given no reason to think that legitimate effort will brighten their future. The law for their forbears may have been an instrument of oppression; the police a source of rudeness or even brutality, rather than of protection. In some slum areas most young men have police records, and a readiness to risk arrest may be considered a sign of manhood.

What this means is that the social context of poverty, and the poorer prospects for those who grow up in it, *both* tend to make socioeconomic deprivation a major cause of crime. A crime prevention strategy which focuses only on punishment, prosecution, and policing is therefore not only insufficient in terms of the theory that is used to justify it, but in addition neglects the cultural factors that must also be taken into account.

Among those who commit crimes there are not only those whose values and perceptions are the result of the influence of deviant social groups such as teenage gangs. There are also those whose deviance is a product of mental illness. There are some people in every social class who act as though they wish to be punished or as though they have determined that their values will be the opposite of those that social authorities lay down, whatever these values may be. For those who value punishment in general or deviance in general to some degree, to a like extent the punishments generally prescribed to deter crime will be ineffective. This illustrates the importance of keeping the extraordinary complexity of criminal motivation in mind.

Crime and Civil Disorders

The importance of group attitudes toward the law and the police, and of the objective obstacles to legitimate success in the slum environment, are illustrated by the civil disorders. These disorders tend to center in ghetto areas whose residents regularly list police behavior—lack of service and protection as well as rudeness and brutality—as primary complaints.

It seems likely that such negative attitudes toward the police and the system of law, and pessimism about the prospects of legitimate success, cannot be remedied through harsher punishment, a strengthening of public prosecutors, or more police. Such measures may help, but they are unlikely by themselves to prevent either individual crime or violent protest. The objective opportunities for the poor, and their attitudes toward the police and the law, must also change before the problems can be solved.

The Policy Challenge

The crime problem confronts society with a number of alternatives. Apprehension and punishment serve as deterrents to crime, as does an increase in police strength and effectiveness. At the same time an enlargement of opportunities, and measures to improve the social context in which crime emerges, are also necessary. Crime is, in other words, an index of the health of the entire social organism.

Chapter VI

Learning, Science, and Art

HOW MUCH ARE THEY ENRICHING SOCIETY?

KNOWLEDGE, intellectual skills and the creative capacity of scientists and artists are an important part of the Nation's wealth. Health, national defense, and the quality of the environment in future years depend on the success of research and education now. So does the future performance of the economy. Some studies have suggested that as much as one-fourth of our growth in per capita income can be traced to increased schooling and as much as one-third to inventions and "advances in knowledge." The decisive productive potential of the supply of knowledge is illustrated by the surprisingly rapid recovery of the German and Japanese economies after the devastation of World War II. However much physical capital had been destroyed, the stock of useful knowledge remained.

This chapter will first attempt to bring together available information on how much Americans are learning. It will then turn to the sources of the knowledge that there is to teach: to the stock of systematic knowledge which we call science, and to the unstructured collection of human wisdom and creativity which we call art.

LEARNING

Exposure to Learning

The average American has spent far more time in school than his parents did. Today, three-fourths of the Americans just old enough to have done so have finished high school—roughly the same proportion that finished the eighth grade in 1929. Today, about 15 percent of Americans in their late twenties have graduated from college—about the same proportion that had graduated from high school at the time of World War I.

In addition there has been an increase in the proportion of each year that the student spends in school. Since 1900, 34 days have been added to the average academic year. Pupils are also absent much less often, so the actual number of days of school attendance per year by the average pupil has increased by more than half.

The difference in years of schooling received by different groups of Americans has at the same time decreased. Among Americans born in 1901 or shortly before, those in the 90th percentile had 13.5 years of schooling, and those in the 10th percentile 2.6 years of schooling, for a difference of almost 11 years. Among those born between 1932 and 1936, those in the 90th percentile had 16.4 years of schooling, and those in the 10th percentile, 8.4 years, for a difference of 8 years. This difference is projected to decline to about 5.5 years for those born between 1956 and 1960. The gap in median years of schooling between whites and Negroes has fallen from an average of 3.4 years for those born in 1901 or before to one-half year for those born between 1942 and 1946, and appears to be narrowing still further.

The amount of resources used to educate each pupil is also increasing. In 1956, there were 27 pupils for each teacher; now there are 24. Teachers have also had more formal training; 93 percent of the teachers now have college degrees, as compared with 78 percent only 13 years ago. The one-room school, commonplace in rural areas as late as World War II, has largely disappeared. Total expenditures per pupil in elementary and secondary public schools increased from $2.25 to $3.43 per day (in constant dollars) between 1954 and 1964. There have also been improvements in curricula, especially in science and mathematics.

It is generally assumed that these increases in the length of schooling and expenditures on education have brought about an increase in the amount children have learned. There is, however, almost no direct evidence on this point—unless it be the evidence that parents often have difficulty with their children's homework. The *Digest of Educational Statistics*, for example, contains over a hundred pages of educational statistics in each annual issue, yet has virtually no information on how much children have learned. The Department of Health, Education, and Welfare has recently encouraged an attempt at a "national assessment" of educational achievement in the United States. This assessment would involve administering tests measuring standard academic skills to a representative sample of Americans of various ages. Such an assessment, if repeated periodically, would yield for the first time a series of estimates of the change taking place in the intellectual skills and knowledge of the population.

Are We Learning More?

In 1870, 20 percent of the white and 80 percent of the Negro population were illiterate. Now only 2.4 percent are deemed illiterate. They are mostly older people and Negroes, and are concentrated mainly in the South. The rate of illiteracy among Americans from 14 to 24 years of age is only about one-half of 1 percent. These facts mark our progress in bringing most Americans up to the rudimentary but critical point of being able to read and write.

What about higher levels of skill and knowledge? Although there is no national assessment of what students are learning, testing is widespread and some clues to changes in test performance of school-age children are available.

The Educational Testing Service recently assembled 186 instances in which comparable tests have been given to large and roughly representative national samples of students at two different times over the past two decades.

In all but 10 of the 186 paired comparisons, the later group performed better than the earlier group. On the average an additional eight percent of the students in the more recent group scored higher than the median student in the old group.[1]

The results that have been described cannot be accepted uncritically; neither can they be casually dismissed. Until better evidence is presented, the tentative judgment must be that American children in the sixties are learning more than their older brothers and sisters learned in the fifties.

This collection of achievement test data also suggests that high school students, and perhaps students in the higher grades generally, have not improved as much as students in the lower grades. Typically, the test comparisons for high schools showed a smaller gain in performance than was usual in the elementary grades. In addition, the Preliminary Scholastic Aptitude Test and the American College Test program, which are given to juniors and seniors in high school, showed no improvement on balance.[2]

One possible reason for this disparity is that the increase in the proportion of teenagers attending high school may have reduced the average level of intellectual ability and cultural background in high schools. The increase in preschool education may also have had a particularly beneficial influence on the lower grades. Television may have at the same time significantly raised the intellectual level of younger children, but seldom stretched the minds of high school students.

---

[1] This amounts to an improvement of one-fifth, assuming a normal distribution of scores. These test results must be interpreted with extreme caution. There is the possibility students are becoming increasingly "test wise" as time goes on, and this might account for the improvement in test scores. Moreover, test results do not measure all types of intellectual achievement. There could have been retrogression along those dimensions of intellectual development that the tests did not measure.

[2] Average scores on the Medical College Admission Test and the Law School Admission Test have been increasing. But this does not show that college students are necessarily learning more, since the sort of students who apply for medical and law school admission may change over time.

How Much More Could We Be Learning?

One way to answer this question is by comparing the performance of American students with those in other countries to see if we are doing as well.

One of the few sources on how well American students do as compared with foreign students is the International Study of Achievement in Mathematics. It deals with only one subject, but this is probably the one in which performance can best be compared among nations with different languages and cultures. The study considered only developed nations, and found that American students had one of the poorest levels of performance of the nations which were studied.

The fact that the United States did badly in this comparison is probably due in part to the fact that a larger proportion of young people go through the secondary education system in the United States than in most other countries. Still, American 13 year olds also did comparatively poorly, and this is an age at which none of the countries concerned have excluded many children from the educational system. Thus, if we contend that American youth have on the average as much aptitude for mathematics as children of other nations, we must conclude that we can do much better than we are doing.

In estimating the potential for improvement in American education, international comparisons are probably less relevant than measured differences in learning among different groups in the United States.

For estimating differences in learning among groups, the two best sources of information are the Armed Forces Qualification Test (with its forbear, the Army General Classification Test), and the tests done for the *Survey of Educational Opportunity* (also called the "Coleman Report") carried out under the Civil Rights Act of 1964.

These tests, like others, inevitably incorporate cultural bias. Verbal performance, for example, tends to be measured in terms of the student's command of literary English or the standard conversation of the majority, not in terms of the special dialects of minorities. Mathematics tests include fractions and compound interest, but rarely deal with the probability of "making a six" in craps. Nonetheless, the tests measure skills which are needed in order to do well in contemporary American society.

The Armed Forces Qualification Test is used to evaluate the trainability of prospective servicemen for military service. Because the proportion of young men who are drafted changes from time to time, place to place, and group to group, the test does not provide entirely satisfactory information. Nonetheless, it shows clearly that Negroes and Southern whites score, on the average, lower than whites from other regions, and Southern Negroes score less well than Northern Negroes. These groups receive, on average, different amounts of schooling, but this difference accounts for only part of the differences in performance.

A 1964 study by the President's Task Force on Manpower Conservation revealed that a majority of young men failing the Armed Forces Qualification Test, white and black alike, were brought up in poverty. Forty percent had never gone beyond eighth grade, four out of five failed to complete high school, and half came from families with five or more children.

The *Survey of Educational Opportunity* was based on a nationwide sample of 564,000 students in grades 1, 3, 6, 9, and 12. The tests covered verbal ability, nonverbal intelligence, reading comprehension, mathematics, and general information in the practical arts, natural sciences, social studies and humanities. With the exception of Oriental American children, the average minority group pupil (Negro, Mexican-American, American Indian, Puerto Rican) scored distinctly lower on these tests than the average white pupil. Students in the South, both white and Negro, scored below students of their own race in the North.

The schooling which the disadvantaged groups had received had apparently done nothing to lessen the gap between them and more fortunate pupils. Their disadvantage was evident from the start of their school experience through grade 12. The relative position of the different groups was about the same for all the grades tested (except in the South, where Negroes fell to a lower relative position in the later grades). This means that in terms of absolute grade level the disadvantaged fell further behind. Negro pupils in the metropolitan Northeast, for example, were 1.6 years below the norm in grade 6 and 3.3 years below the norm in grade 12.

The Armed Forces Qualification Test and the *Survey of Educational Opportunity* thus show that persons from both poorer groups and poorer areas performed less well on achievement tests, and that the existing pattern of schooling does not compensate for the initial handicap entailed in being brought up in a disadvantaged group or area.

If talented individuals do not get a full education, the Nation is obviously not developing its capacities as much as it could. And as the chapter on "Social Mobility" showed, only half of those who are in the top ability quintile, but from families in the lowest socioeconomic quartile, go to college, whereas 95 percent of the equally able students from the top socioeconomic quartile go to college. Socioeconomic status also has a major effect on college attendance at other ability levels.

If high school graduates from all socioeconomic levels went to college in the same proportion as high school graduates of the same ability level in the top socioeconomic quartile, more than half a million additional students would enter college each year. This would increase the number who attended college from each high school graduating class by about one-half.

If the environmental and social handicaps of poor children could be overcome, and the elementary and secondary education they receive improved, an even larger number of high school graduates could profit from a college education.

We have seen that American students did less well in mathematics than students in a number of other countries, and that the pattern of results in the Armed Forces Qualification Test and the *Survey of Educational Opportunity* implied that there is an untapped reservoir of intellectual capacity in the Nation's disadvantaged groups and areas. It is also clear that those young people from poor families who do nonetheless score well on achievement tests are much less likely to enter college than those who come from a higher socioeconomic level. Thus there is no doubt that the Nation has failed to take full advantage of its children's capacity to learn.

The Policy Challenge

The greatest challenge to American education today is to find effective ways of helping low income children learn the basic intellectual skills so that they can be more successful in school and compete more successfully for jobs and rewarding positions in the community when they become adults.

How much a child learns depends upon his mother's diet before he was born, his own nutrition and health, his access to books, and the psychological and intellectual influences in the home. Most psychologists seem to agree that the preschool years are a period of particularly rapid development, and that attitudes acquired in these years can have enduring effects. Even after he reaches school age, a child typically spends only one-third of his working hours in school. Television programs and conversations with parents and playmates take up much of a child's time. The motivation to learn is obviously important, and there is every reason to believe it is decisively influenced by the home environment.

Some of the findings in the *Survey of Educational Opportunity* suggest the importance of the educational impact of factors outside of school. The *Survey* found that the socioeconomic status of a child's parents, and of his classmates, were major determinants of a student's academic performance. Once the impact of the socioeconomic status of parents and peers had been accounted for, such differences in quality of schooling as were observed and measured explained very little of the remaining variation in student performance.[3] The only observed school characteristic that had a significant effect was the verbal ability of its teachers, and this effect was much smaller than that of socioeconomic status of parents and classmates.

Despite the limitations of the *Survey* the conclusion that a child's socioeconomic environment is an important determinant of how much he learns is almost certainly right. This conclusion, in turn, suggests that we cannot take full advantage of the potential for learning simply by spending more on schools. Higher incomes and better jobs for parents may have more influence on their children's learning than any "compensation" which can be given to the children themselves. Better television programing and help for parents in how to talk with and stimulate their own children may also be important. Improved housing arrangements which give children from poor families the opportunity to attend schools and live in neighborhoods with children of different social and economic status may also be of crucial importance.

Nevertheless, it is clear that schools could do far more to stimulate and foster the curiosity and creativity of children—not just poor children, but all children. We must somehow find a way to do two things. First, we need to channel more resources into education especially in areas where the needs are very high in relation to the tax base and present spending. It takes money to attract sensitive, intelligent, and highly trained people into teaching and education administration, and to replace rat-infested old schools, especially in the center cities, with attractive convenient structures.

But resources alone will not solve the problems of American education. A new spirit of acceptance of change and desire for improvement is needed. Progressive industries often spend 5 to 10 percent of their funds on research and development. But expenditures on education research and development are now miniscule, perhaps a half of 1 percent of the total education budget.

Furthermore, much "research and development" in education consists of small projects having little impact on actual learning in the schools. There is a need for major departures, for developing whole new curricula and approaches to education, for trying the new approaches with real children and real schools. This kind of effort is expensive, by the present standards of education research, although

---

[3] The *Survey* did not measure the quality of schools well and its conclusions are subject to varying interpretations. The conclusion that the socioeconomic status of the families of a student's classmates is an important determinant of a student's performance could be interpreted as evidence that differences in the quality of schooling are important, because high status parents usually want and can afford to live in neighborhoods with good schools. Since variations in the quality of schooling were measured only partially and crudely in the *Survey*, it is possible that the average socioeconomic status of the families of the students in a school measures the quality of that school better than the explicit measures of school quality used in the *Survey*.

not by the standards of military and industrial research and development.

But even a major effort to find more effective methods in education through research and development will not be sufficient unless the schools as a whole adopt a new attitude toward change. School systems must learn to see themselves as continuous laboratories trying new things, evaluating results, and making changes.

SCIENCE

The advance of science has an effect on the Nation's capacity to produce more goods and services, better health, and a stronger defense. Our society also values scientific truth for its own sake. And because it is clear that the state of a nation's science is related to its productivity, the health of its people, and even to national security, Americans are concerned whenever any other nation excels us in an important area of scientific capability.

Resources Devoted to Science

What is the state of American science and how much are we adding to the stock of systematic knowledge? Unfortunately, useful measures of scientific productivity do not exist.

A frequent measure of our scientific capital is the number of scientists and the amount of resources devoted to scientific pursuits. Between 1950 and 1965 the number of scientists and engineers nearly doubled, reaching about a million and a half in the latter year. About a million were engineers, a half a million scientists. This increase in the number of scientists and engineers was 4.5 times the rate of growth of the total labor force. The number of scientists and engineers getting doctorates has doubled in the last 10 years.

Between 1953 and 1965 the Nation's research and development expenditures increased fourfold, from 5.2 billion to 20.5 billion. This means that these expenditures increased at a compound annual rate of 12 percent per year, and that the percent of the Gross National Product used for these purposes rose from 1.4 to 3.0 percent. No other nation comes close to devoting a similar proportion of its resources to scientific research and development.

The Diversity of Science

Three hundred years ago all experimental sciences were grouped together in one specialty called "natural philosophy." An individual could attempt to master almost all important scientific knowledge. In 1958, the National Science Foundation counted 120 subfield groupings and 142 groupings in 1968. The number of particular specialties increased even faster: 695 specialties were listed in 1958, 1,235 in 1968.

This increase of specialization does not measure the pace of scientific advance. Classifications and new specialties are sometimes created for reasons unrelated to the growth of knowledge. Nonetheless, the statistics on the increasing diversity and division of labor in science reflect the rapid growth of scientific exploration and knowledge.

The Advance of Technology

The remarkable advances of industrial technology in recent years are too obvious to need documentation. Television, supersonic jets, computers, nuclear power and many other advances have revolutionized our lives and made possible feats, like trips around the moon, that earlier generations thought sheer fantasy. Whereas the *Mayflower* took 2 months to cross the Atlantic, in the 1890's it took 1 week, in the 1930's a day, and now about 7 hours. But advancing technology has also created problems for society—noise, congestion, pollution, and the like.

Some insight into the level of technological achievement in the United States can be obtained from what is called the "technological balance of payments." This is an accounting of payments foreigners have made to us for the use of patented techniques or technical expertise, minus our payments for their patents and technical expertise.[4] The United States enjoys a huge surplus in the technological balance of payments, and this surplus appears to be growing. Our surplus was $311 million in 1956 and $1,097 million in 1965. The ratio of our payments to our receipts was one to seven in 1956 and one to nine in 1965. If the transfers within multinational firms are left out, our surplus is still growing; it rose from $110 million in 1956 to $235 million in 1965.

These striking figures on our technological lead can easily mislead us. Science is international, and any major scientific achievement is likely to be of mixed ancestry. Moreover, many scientists have come to this country from other lands. Although the "brain drain" increases the inequality of income among nations, it is nonetheless an encouraging indicator about the state of American science.

The Policy Challenge

The main challenge presented by the state of American science is the need to lay the foundations for a science policy. We are confronted with burgeoning advance that offers great promise. Can we formulate policies that will nurture our invaluable scientific resources and ensure the fulfillment of prospects that lie ahead?

The competition for public resources will almost certainly be more intense, either between science and other programs, or between different scentific endeavors. The Nation will also continue to find itself

---

[4] This is not an ideal measure because of problems of definition and the bias against basic science.

at the center of controversies concerning the condition and needs of world science.

If there is almost sure to be more heat generated by issues of science policy in the future, ways must be found to generate more light. Priorities in science could be laid out more systematically, and farther in advance. Issues involving such priorities could be exposed to wider public debate. The very unpredictability of scientific breakthroughs could be made the basis for more rational development of scientific manpower, institutions, and communications with an emphasis on keeping these resources flexible.

The international character of the scientific enterprise poses a special challenge. The United States, as we have seen, spends a larger *percentage* of its income on scientific research and development than do other countries. One possible explanation for this is that some of the benefits of scientific advance are readily available to any nation in the world. For example, people of any country can take advantage of such medical advances as heart transplants. Because of its size and affluence, the United States gets a larger share of the benefit of a basic scientific advance than other countries, and therefore has an incentive to spend more of its national income on basic research. Even the biggest countries do not, however, reap all of the benefits of the basic research they finance. Thus the world as a whole probably tends to spend too little on basic science.

The benefits of basic research are international, and worldwide cooperation in science is essential. A cooperative recognition of the universality of basic science could benefit all mankind.

ART

Artistic creativity and its appreciation are an important part of our national life. There is art not only in museums, theaters, opera houses, and books but in every aspect of life—in cooking, dress and industrial design. Although this section concentrates on the conventionally most professional and "highbrow" forms of art, we must not forget that this is only a small part of the total and may not be the most important.

Access to Art

Access to many forms of art is easier today than it has ever been before. Modern technologies of communication and transportation have given the entire population an access to a variety of art forms that could in an earlier age have been open only to a privileged few. Even the most fortunate in earlier periods could not possibly have heard as wide a variety of symphonies, or seen such a diversity of drama, as the connoisseur of records and motion pictures can enjoy today.

This improvement in the accessibility of art has continued even in recent years. Twenty-five years ago almost no one owned a television set: by 1952, 30 percent of the households owned at least one set, and this percentage rose to 67 percent in 1955, 88 percent in 1960, and 94 percent in 1967.

Notwithstanding the obvious shortcomings in television programing, the growth in the number of television sets has given more Americans an access to at least some serious attempts at artistic expression. National Educational Television's 148 stations now reach almost all metropolitan areas, and surveys have shown that the NET audience about doubled between 1961 and 1966, by which time it reached over 6 million homes and an estimated 14 million viewers weekly, apart from school programs. Of 260 hours of programming supplied last year to NET's affiliates, about half or more were in the field of art and culture.

Television is, to be sure, only one of the technologies that has made art more accessible. Even such an old technology as that involved in making books has changed with the "paperback revolution," which has made books more accessible to millions of Americans. This development, along with expanding incomes, increased education, and other factors, has brought about a 90-percent increase in the number of new books and editions between 1960 and 1967, and a 65-percent increase in books classified in the arts or humanities. These increases considerably exceed the rates of growth of population and income.

Improved methods of transportation and increased incomes have also widened the range of possible artistic experience for many Americans by facilitating foreign travel. In 1929 about half a million Americans traveled abroad, but in 1967 almost three and a half million did so.

New technologies have not only widened the access to art, but also permitted new forms of artistic expression, from films to new kinds of sculpture and music.

The Performing Arts

At the same time that technology and economic advance have improved the accessibility of many types of art, they have also created problems for other art forms, especially for those involving live performances. There is evidence that live performances of certain kinds are not increasing in proportion to the growth of population and the economy, and in some cases are perhaps even in an absolute decline.

The Broadway theaters are the largest single part of the American theater, and they have been keeping records in a consistent way longer than other theaters. These records reveal that Broadway attendance has not expanded in proportion to our population or economic growth. The Broadway theater reached its peak quite some time ago, probably about 1925. No new Broadway theater has been built since 1928.[5] There has been no clear trend in attendance since World War II, and there clearly has not been enough of an increase to offset rapidly rising costs. Since 1950, ticket prices have risen only half as much as costs. Though a few "hits" make great profits, the Broadway theater as a whole is in serious financial difficulty.

The off-Broadway theater grew rapidly from the late 1940's until the midsixties, but it has an attendance of about one million, compared with seven million for Broadway. More recently, the off-Broadway theater has suffered, too; the number of productions is now smaller than it was in 1961-62.

There has been little or no growth in the number of professional symphony orchestras since 1950. In 1967 there were 28 entirely professional symphony orchestras playing for seasons ranging from 22 to 52 weeks. There are about twice as many "metropolitan" orchestras, mainly professional but having smaller budgets, and a large number of partially amateur community orchestras.

Chamber music groups are generally less well organized than symphony orchestras. Receipts from ticket sales to the small halls appropriate for chamber groups are generally low, and the cost of the individual performer relatively high. Some orchestras are organizing chamber groups to achieve the advantages of a longer season for some of their members.

Opera is perhaps the most vulnerable of the arts because it is easily the most expensive, requiring large casts, an orchestra, a chorus, and a ballet company as well as expensive scenery and costumes. The only major opera companies are the Metropolitan, the New York City Opera, the Chicago Lyric Opera, and the San Francisco Opera. There are about 40 other professional and semiprofessional organizations, but they usually give no more than 25 performances in a year. Estimating total attendance at these performances requires a good deal of guesswork, but the figure has been placed at less than 2 million in 1963-64.

Ballet as a separate artistic undertaking is characterized by high costs in many of the same areas as opera. Annual attendance for dance performances is estimated at less than 1 million, with dance tours showing a marked relative growth in popularity since 1952. At the present time, however, there is little chance to see a professional dance company perform any place except in one of the largest cities or in a college town.

Notwithstanding the paucity of information in this area, it does seem very likely that there is no "cultural boom" where direct attendance at live performances is involved. The rate of growth in such performances is probably slower than that of the economy as a whole, and

---

[5] Unless Lincoln Center is counted.

expenditures on these art forms have certainly not risen at anything like the rate at which expenditures on science and education have increased.

Vulnerability of the Performing Arts

To some extent, the relative decline in live artistic performances is probably a natural result of the development of modern communications technology. The new technologies offer a less expensive substitute for live performance.

But there is another factor at work. One explanation of the slow growth of audience participation in the performing arts is the tendency for this participation to become even relatively more expensive as the economy advances. There is little increase in productivity per worker in the performing arts: a string quartet continues to require four performers. In the economy in general productivity increases regularly, and so then do wage levels. Since this does not happen in the performing arts, someone must make sacrifices. If it is not the public or the patrons, it will be the artists themselves, who will have to choose other careers or forego higher incomes.

This systematic tendency for the relative cost of live performance to rise is made somewhat less serious by the technological improvements in ways of disseminating culture, such as by phonograph records, motion pictures, and television, providing substitutes for the audiences and additional earnings for some performers. But if there is presumably also a need to enjoy culture at first hand, these technological developments do not altogether fill the gap from the audiences' point of view. From the performers' point of view, the fact that only a relatively small number can expect careers in the media may be discouraging.

There is another cultural sector, where the problem of productivity can be considered not to exist at all. This is what we might call amateur or subsistence culture: artistic work carried on by the artist primarily for his own enjoyment. Increased incomes may allow more of this, as growth of amateur community symphonies, for example, seems to show. Sometimes amateur efforts can create or enlarge a commercial audience, as with rock music.

The probable long run tendency for a relative decline in certain types of live performances does not automatically indicate a "social" or "public" problem. Nevertheless, live performances are needed to give the typical performer (or composer or playwright) a chance to develop. The quality of records, motion pictures and television could decline if live performances fell off beyond some point, since the lack of this large testing and training opportunity could become critical.

The performing arts indirectly benefit others besides members of live audiences in other ways as well. Their quality is tied up with the capacity to educate, and probably also the capacity to communicate. The cultural inheritance of a nation is also a source of important values in a civilized society—understanding, appreciation, and respect for other people. Finally, the taste for art is in part an acquired taste: those who have a broader cultural experience tend to have the greatest concern for art. The demand for art might be greater if the opportunities to enjoy it were more numerous. These arguments suggest that the prospect of a relative decline in live performances is a matter of general public concern, and something to keep in mind in any assessment of the condition of American society.

Chapter VII

Participation and Alienation
WHAT DO WE NEED TO LEARN?

THE PRECEDING CHAPTERS neglect many of the Nation's major concerns. They have, for example, scarcely mentioned the divisions in our society which separate young and old, black and white, left and right. Yet these divisions trouble many Americans, and help explain the demonstrations at universities, the disorders in cities, and the manifestations of racist and extremist strength. The preceding chapters have similarly neglected the controversies about court decisions defining our individual liberties, demands for "democratic participation" in the organizational life of the society, and the concern some Americans have about the viability and stability of family life.

The most notable of the problems that have been neglected are those that concern the functioning of our social and political institutions. To the extent that these institutions have promoted health, deterred crime, and the like, their achievements belong in preceding chapters. But we also care about *how* we combine our efforts to achieve our goals, about our loyalty toward our institutions, about our attitudes toward each other, and about the implications of our social and political institutions for the future of the Nation. However good our health or high our incomes, we would not be satisfied with institutions that failed to respect individual rights, allow democratic participation, provide congenial group affiliations, or insure the survival and orderly development of our society.

Unfortunately, it is concerns such as these that we know least about. It is more difficult to assess the extent to which our political and social institutions satisfy democratic values, or prevent alienation, than it is to assess the level of health, income, or crime.

Therefore, we can do little more than ask the right questions. Yet it is important that these questions be asked. If assessments of the state of the Nation take account only of those variables that are readily measurable, our social priorities and public policies will be distorted. It will not be possible to obtain the needed information in the future unless the questions are asked now.

Since the primary purpose of this report is to examine the condition of American society, the questions should pertain to the basic functions our social and political institutions perform, rather than to their structures or characteristics.

One purpose our institutions should surely serve is that of protecting our individual liberties—one of the first ideals of our Nation. Democratic processes are meaningless if citizens do not have a large measure of freedom, particularly freedom to dissent from the policy of the Government and the views of the majority. Thus the first section of this chapter asks questions about the degrees of "Freedom and Constraint" in American life.

In a modern democracy, individual liberty cannot be the privilege of a few: It must be available on an equal basis to every law-abiding citizen. A system in which some stand above the law, while others are denied its protection, is repugnant to the idea of justice. Equality before the law in turn implies that every citizen have access to public services on an equal basis according to law. The citizens must also be able to influence public policy, and in the aggregate influence it decisively, or they are not truly free. There must be meaningful voting, and the vote of each citizen must count equally. The second section of this chapter therefore raises questions about the extent to which the ideal of "Equality and Justice" is being realized.

A people may enjoy freedom, and a just and equal political system, yet lack any sense of community. Many may be alienated, not only from the Nation, but also from their families, neighborhoods, and other social groups. Some degree of alienation and disunity is acceptable in a society that values individual freedom, and the alienated may be creative and bring about reforms which benefit society as a whole. But if alienation becomes so pervasive that all sense of community is lost, the result can be disaster.

The degree of alienation also depends on the functioning of all the social groups in the society. A person may be alienated because of the failure of his family, the shortcomings of his neighborhood, the lack of a congenial club, or the policies of the National Government.

Thus the third section of this chapter, on "Community and Alienation," asks how strong are the bonds which maintain our relationships to social institutions, from the family to the National Government. Here we encounter what many Americans find the most worrisome questions of contemporary life: How serious are the divisions in our society? How can we bridge the generation gap that divides families and universities, and the racial and ideological differences that divide neighborhood and Nation?

QUESTIONS ABOUT FREEDOM AND CONSTRAINT

It is a sign of the profound value placed on freedom that many use this word to describe a great many of the things they want. Better education, more goods and services, and higher incomes give people the freedom to do things they could not have done before. But we are discussing freedom here in its most ancient and basic sense: those rights that allow an individual to use his time, talents, and resources in whatever way he pleases, so long as this does not interfere with the rights of others.

Freedom of Expression

Democracy cannot be meaningful if those who disagree with the policy of the government have no opportunity to persuade their fellow citizens to vote it out of office. Thus freedom of expression, both for individuals and for groups, is absolutely indispensable to a democratic society.[1] We must therefore ask particularly about the freedom to express dissenting and unpopular views.

There can be little doubt that court decisions in the recent past have expanded the legal protection for free speech. Important as these legal developments have been, they are by no means the whole story. Freedom of expression can be restricted not only by government officials, but also by popular intolerance. However, the extent of such intolerance is not known.

There is some evidence that a majority of Americans on occasion have wanted to deny free speech to their fellow citizens, and that this disposition has been more prevalent among the rank and file than among community leaders. In the period of the Red scare of the early fifties, only 27 percent of Americans thought that an admitted Communist should be allowed to make a speech in their communities; but 51 percent of community leaders felt such a speech should be permitted. Among the general population, only about 37 percent thought that a person who wanted to speak against religion should be allowed to speak in their communities. Again, community leaders were more tolerant; 64 percent of them believed such a speech should be allowed.[2]

There is a need for tolerance not only in national political forums, but also in daily life. How much tolerance of dissent is there in our schools, factories, and offices? We do not know, but some approximate answers could be obtained, as one study shows.

In this study, representative samples of persons in the United States, the United Kingdom, Germany, Italy, and Mexico were asked about the extent to which they had as students felt free to discuss unfair

---
[1] If there is freedom of expression and organization, there is automatically a good deal of religious freedom as well.
[2] Samuel Stouffer, *Communism, Conformity, and Civil Liberties* (New York: Doubleday & Co., 1954), pp. 26–44.

TABLE 1.—*Freedom to discuss unfair treatment in school or to disagree with teacher, by nation*

Percent who remember they felt	U.S. (percent)	U.K. (percent)	Germany (percent)	Italy (percent)	Mexico (percent)
Free	45	35	34	29	40
Uneasy	23	18	24	19	16
Better not to talk to teacher	25	41	30	36	39
Don't know, don't remember, and other	8	6	12	16	5
Total	100	100	100	100	100
Total number	969	963	953	907	783

SOURCE: Almond and Verba, *The Civic Culture*, p. 332.

TABLE 2.—*Freedom to participate in school discussions and debates, by nation*

Percent who remember they felt	U.S. (percent)	U.K. (percent)	Germany (percent)	Italy (percent)	Mexico (percent)
Could and did participate	40	16	12	11	15
Could but did not participate	15	8	5	4	21
Could not participate	34	68	68	56	54
Don't know and other	11	8	15	29	10
Total	100	100	100	100	100
Total number	969	963	953	907	783

SOURCE: Almond and Verba, *The Civic Culture*, p. 333.

treatment in school or disagree with the teacher, and whether they had participated in school debates on political and social issues. As tables 1 and 2 reveal, American respondents were more likely than those in any of the other countries surveyed to say that they had felt free to disagree with their teachers, discuss unfair treatment with them, and participate in school discussions and debates. Americans were also more likely to be consulted about job decisions and to protest job decisions than those in most of the countries surveyed.

The lack of information about the extent of our liberties may suggest that we are not as vigilant about the state of our freedom as we purport to be. Here we can do little more than pose the question of how well the Nation is protecting the individual rights its rhetoric emphasizes. But the question is itself important. If it is asked more often, we will in time be able to provide better answers.

QUESTIONS ABOUT EQUALITY AND JUSTICE

Equal treatment is a cornerstone of our society. We believe in equality before the law: The judicial system must deal equally with the great and the small, or there is no justice. We believe in the right to equal access to public services: The administrative apparatus should treat all citizens in the same way, according to law. We believe in the one-man-one-vote ideal: The political system should give each citizen equal access to the electoral process, so that no group can wield poltical power disproportionate to its numbers. These ideas of equality and justice are not only enshrined in our rhetoric; they are essential to the viability and integrity of our democratic processes. If those who oppose the existing leadership cannot depend on the protection of the courts, or equal access to public services, or voting power comparable to their number, democracy is threatened.

Justice in the Courts

A democratic society must always ask whether everyone accused has a right to counsel and all of the other requisites of a fair trial; whether justice is so long delayed it is in effect denied; whether every citizen has equal access to publicly provided services.

The American system of justice, with its ancient roots in the common law, its elaborate rights of appeal, and thoroughgoing system of judicial review, is properly a source of national pride. Yet there is evidence that some suffer rough and ready justice at the hands of the police; that some are tried without adequate counsel; that publicity and prejudice may sometimes prevent a jury from rendering justice. In some parts of the country, the punishment of those accused of rape has varied with their race and the race of their victims.

One reason why so little is known about the exact extent of such inequities in our system of justice is that virtually *any* such wrong is a matter of great seriousness. It can result in the impeachment of a judge, or the expulsion or loss of pay of a policeman. Because so much is at stake, it is extremely difficult to collect information on shortcomings as a matter of statistical routine. Yet, if we believe in justice, we are obliged to ask to whom it has been denied.

Access and Redress in Large Organizations

A growing group of Americans, especially among the young and the black, are intensely concerned about the relationship between the individual and the large bureaucracies. They are concerned about the relationship between the citizen and the police force, the student and the university, the claimant and the insurance company, the welfare client and the public assistance office, the tenant and the housing authority, the employee and the hierarchy.

The concern about the relationship between the individual and the bureaucracy is coming from diverse segments of the political spectrum. Historically, those on the right have been most anxious about the evils of bureaucracy and most enthusiastic about decentralization. But recently, the "new left" seems on its way to putting democratic participation in large organizations, including some forms of decentralization, above the left's traditional advocacy of central planning and the nationalization of industry.

The problem is this: How can the individual citizen, especially the citizen who is lacking in education, influence, and self-confidence, get the services he should expect from large bureaucracies, or get redress from the wrongs they may commit against him? The person accused of a crime has recourse to an elaborate system of justice replete with features designed to protect those unjustly accused. But the citizen who cannot get the police protection he needs, or who suffers rude treatment from the police, may find that the courts are irrelevant, or so costly and cumbersome that they are of no use. The man who can't get a license to work, or get a public utility bill corrected, or have an insurance claim processed promptly, may not have the option of turning to the courts. He may know that "you can't fight city hall," or influence a large corporation.

It is always possible to complain, and complaints sometimes help. Yet all too often complaints get lost in a snarl of red tape. This is especially true for the person who lacks education, or experience with large organizations, or who lacks the stamina, resources, and gall needed to make a large issue out of what the bureaucracy may take to be a small matter.

Today, as never before in our history, people seem to be at the mercy of huge, impersonal bureaucracies. Even when large bureaucracies function efficiently, there still may be resistance and resentment. People want to be treated personally and humanely. They do not want to be only a cog in a machine. The courtesy of an explanation, or a sympathetic ear, may make all the difference.

The expansion of government services, both at Federal and local levels, has increased the multiplicity of offices and agencies with which the citizen must deal. Millions of Americans think of their government as distant and unresponsive, though paradoxically many seem to think the city government more remote than the Federal.

The decline of the political machine typical of the 19th century city may also be a factor. Corrupt as these machines were, they nonetheless were responsive to the needs of many of the immigrants from Europe, and helped assimilate them into American life. The mid-20th century immigrants to the city are mainly Negroes from rural areas of the South who have not been assimilated into the political structure nor had the personal relationships with the city government that the political machines afforded earlier immigrants.

The difficulty of the relationships between bureaucracies and Negroes is illustrated in table 3. Whereas 87 percent of the whites expect "equal treatment" by administrative officials, only 49 percent of the Negroes do. Negroes are also less likely to feel that administrative officials will pay attention to their point of view, less likely to expect equal treatment from the police, and less likely to think the Government or the Congress pays much attention to what people think.

TABLE 3.—*Responsiveness of governmental officials*

	Total	White	Negro
Percent who expect equal treatment in administrative office*	83% (970)	87% (866)	49% (100)
Percent who expect equal treatment from the police*	85% (970)	88% (866)	60% (100)
Percent who expect administrative official to pay attention to their point of view.*	48% (970)	50% (856)	30% (100)
Percent who expect police to pay attention to their point of view*	56% (970)	58% (866)	36% (100)
Percent who feel elections make the government pay much or some attention.**	89.2% (1450)	90% (1291)	83.8% (148)
Percent who feel most Congressmen pay much or some attention to what people think.**	79.2% (1450)	79.3% (1291)	78.4% (148)

NOTE.—Numbers in parentheses refer to the bases upon which percentages are calculated.
SOURCE: *Almond and Verba, *The Civic Culture*, 1960.
**Survey Research Center, University of Michigan, *Election Survey*, 1964.

A study of the attitudes of Southern whites and Negroes, on what they would do about the problem of a dangerous school crossing, again shows the Negro's sense of uneasiness in dealing with officialdom. Though Negro responses indicated they would be about as likely to take action about a dangerous school crossing as whites, they were less likely to deal with the official directly, and more likely to speak to "influential" private persons. Whereas 49 percent of the whites would talk to the school officials, only 33 percent of the Negroes would. Though only 1 percent of the whites would talk to an influential private person, 8 percent of the Negroes would.

We need to consider a wide variety of new options that will improve participation and help individuals to deal with bureaucracies. Many things can be done. We must consider the merits of ombudsmen or independent investigators who can look into citizen complaints against administrative actions; neighborhood city halls that can bring local government closer to the people; neighborhood service centers that help people find their way to the right agency; consumer protection units; expanded legal aid for the poor; improvement in administrative law, so that the protection of the courts can be broadened; decentralization of police forces, schools, and other governmental functions; effective employee grievance procedures; councils of student representation in university communities, so that student reactions can effectively reach faculty and administration; and informal networks of communication that tell the administrator what his clients are thinking.

Large organizations are a fixture in today's world. How to keep them from colliding with the individual need for identity and participation is a complex problem. It will take a great deal of study to understand this problem, and probably a wide variety of policies to deal with it.

Political Inequities

Universal suffrage, with one vote for each citizen, is one of the requisites of a system in which every individual, whatever his economic or social status, has an equal voice. As recent Supreme Court decisions about "reapportionment" suggest, there is in our constitutional and democratic ethic a concern that each group of citizens have the opportunity to play a role proportionate to its numbers.

Are any groups denied the role in the political system to which their numbers should entitle them?

In some Southern States, most Negroes have historically been denied the right to vote, and the proportion of Negroes registered in these States is still often a great deal smaller than the proportion of whites that are registered. Such inequities are an affront to democracy. Yet it is also significant that these differences in registration rates are steadily getting smaller, partly because of the Civil Rights Acts of recent years, and that in the Northern States Negro registration rates are not much different from those of whites.

There are also distinct differences in the proportion of the *total* population that is registered in the Nation's major cities. A study of 104 major cities showed that rates of voter registration were greater than 90 percent in some cities (such as Detroit, Seattle, and Minneapolis), and less than 70 percent in others (such as Baltimore, Newark, and New York). If literacy tests, methods of purging registration rolls, and inconvenient arrangements for registration are among the factors that account for these differences, they have distinct implications for the distribution of power among different socioeconomic groups.

There is also the question of the fairness of the apportionment of state legislatures and state congressional delegations, but again there is a clear trend toward more equal representation. Gerrymandering also appears to be declining, though this defies accurate measurement.

Insofar as the right to vote and apportionment are concerned, the situation is one of distinct, if not rapid, improvement.

Political power, however, involves more than the right to vote. It can require, among other things, money to finance campaigns, effective political organization, and lobbying or other pressure on the officeholder between elections. In many cases a group will have a major influence on public policy only if it is organized.

Although America has been called a nation of joiners, the fact remains that most Americans do not belong to any organization that represents them in the political system. Only one American in 25 reports membership in an explicitly political club or organization, and only 24 percent report belonging to any organization that they consider to be involved in political or governmental affairs. Only 57 percent report belonging to a voluntary association of any kind, including religious groups. A number of surveys indicate that less than 8 percent attend any political meetings or rallies.

Thus most Americans are without any organizational affiliations that would give them an organized voice in the governmental process.

The frequent lack of significant organized representation for major groups should not be surprising. When a large group of citizens has some common interest or purpose to seek in the political arena, the typical *individual* in that group often finds that it is *not* in his self-interest to contribute his money or time to an organization that attempts to further that common interest. He would get the benefits of any legislation that the organization succeeded in getting passed whether he contributed to that organization or not. And the typical individual in a large group could not by himself be decisive in determining whether or not the desired legislation would be passed. Thus he has little incentive to support an organization working in his political interest, and may very well not do so. The voluntary association seeking favorable legislation for a large group is in a position analogous to that of a government, in that it produces a service that cannot usually be sold in the market, yet it lacks the power to collect taxes, which governments (however popular their policies) require. Accordingly, we cannot assume that every large group of citizens will organize whenever its interests are threatened.

Industries with a small number of large firms will, because the resources are great and the number that need to be organized is small, usually be able to establish trade associations to further their political and other interests. Similarly, some professions, such as medicine, are well organized in part because each doctor can get professional advantages from joining his medical association. Labor unions can sometimes confer some similar benefits through grievance procedures and shop stewards, and often have the benefit of "union shop" provisions as well. Some farm organizations restrict the benefits of their cooperatives and mutual insurance companies to their members, thereby making it more advantageous for farmers to join.

Whereas some groups have the benefit of organization for reasons such as these, other groups, whose interests should have as much claim to attention, do not have these organizational advantages. This introduces an important inequality into our political system, which explains some of the unevenness in governmental attention to different problems.

This inequality particularly affects those with the least income and education. A survey by the National Opinion Research Center found that 52 percent of those with an income over $7,000 belonged to some voluntary association, but only 24 percent of those with an income under $2,000 did. Some 53 percent of the professionals, proprietors, managers, and officials belonged to voluntary associations, but only 32 percent of the skilled laborers, and 21 percent of the unskilled. Forty-two percent of farm owners belonged to such organizations but only 13 percent of farm laborers.

Organizational inequities such as these help us understand the paradoxical strength of "special interests" in a democratic system formally designed to treat everyone alike.

How can the groups with the least organized power assert their interests against those with the most? Enlightened public officials can help. A government can set up an office of consumer affairs, or an agency for migrant workers, and so on. But, in the end, can the problem be solved unless we organize the weak, or weaken the strong?

QUESTIONS ABOUT COMMUNITY AND ALIENATION

The concern about social division and alienation in American society seems greater now than it has been for some time. The rising tempo of protest, especially among the young and the Negro, and the recent manifestations of right-wing discontent, have prompted some Americans to ask why the Nation faces these divisions now.

There are undoubtedly many reasons. The sharp differences about the war probably explain some of the division. Another factor is our growing affluence and new social legislation which lift the expectations of some people and, at the same time, arouse resentment and fear of change among others. A complete analysis of social cohesion would also have to consider, among other things, the ways children are brought up and educated, and the effectiveness of society's mechanisms for mediating and resolving disputes. It would also have to do justice to the positive functions of alienation and division, as sources of innovation and reform.

The alienation from the university, neighborhood, and family may well be of greater concern than the national political divisions. This alienation suggests one of the most fundamental causes of national division—the lack of satisfactory group relationships. People need a sense of belonging, a feeling of community, in some small social group. If such associations are lacking, they will feel alienated; they will have a tendency either to "cop out" of the central life of the society, or else try to reverse the direction of the society by extreme or even violent methods. The more numerous and stronger the social ties that bind an individual to the social order, the more likely he is to feel an attachment to the society, and work within existing rules to improve it.

We then need to ask questions about some of the principal social relationships in the society, and particularly the family, the neighborhood, and the voluntary association.

The Effects of Marital Status

The need for social relationships may be seen in the association between marital status and health. Married people have distinctly lower death rates and lower rates of suicide, alcoholism, and mental illness, than those who have never married or whose marriages have been disrupted by death or divorce.

With the important factors of age, race, and sex accounted for, differentials in death rates by marital status are very great. For every age, race, and sex, married persons have the lowest death rates. This cannot be explained by any difficulties those who are ill might have in getting or keeping a spouse, for the death rates for widowed persons, at all ages and for both sexes, exceed those of the married. Nor are the differences in suicide rates large enough to account for the differences in mortality rates.

Such statistical associations are particularly important here because they illustrate the pervasive and far-reaching consequences close social relationships can have. They add plausibility to the observations which suggest that alienation from society often reflects a lack of satisfactory relationships in small, primary groups, rather than solely global or national developments, and they show the need to inquire into the functioning of all types of social groups.

The Condition of the Family

The family has undergone profound changes in modern times. It was once the basic unit of society—the source of cohesion and security, the unit of economic activity, the means of education and recreation. Today, many of the functions of the family are performed by other institutions, from the Social Security Administration to the school.

The change in the structure and role of the family has had two important consequences. First, young but unmarried adults have had less family affiliation in recent times than in earlier periods. For many Americans now between 18 and 22, the college or university is *in loco parentis*. For some others, a hippie community may play the role the extended family served in earlier periods. Neither the college nor the communities of drop-outs bring different generations together on the intimate terms the extended family once did, nor do they provide the same kind of emotional security and support.

The second consequence is that changes in the family as an institution are sometimes read as signs of the collapse of family life. Thus, increases in divorce rates suggest to some that the value put upon family life is declining, yet the proportion of the population that is married has been increasing.

Between 1940 and 1965 the proportion of the population, after age-adjustment, that is married increased by 7.5 percent, but the proportion divorced increased only 1.3 percent. Those with disrupted marriages tend to marry again, and fewer stay single. Longer life expectancy means that marriage partners have a longer life together, much of it without the obligations of young children. We need much better information on what such changes mean for our well-being and the strength of our institutions.

The Negro family has suffered adversities going back to the days of slavery. A large percentage of Negro children live in disrupted families. In 1965, about 38 percent of the Nation's Negro children did not live with both parents, whereas only 10 percent of white children were in that situation. About twice as many nonwhite children were living with their fathers only, four times as many with their mothers only, and five times as many with neither parent.

A substantial part of this difference is due to the greater rate of illegitimacy in the Negro population. In 1965, 1.2 percent of single white women had a child, but 9.8 percent, over eight times as large a proportion, of the nonwhite women did. This difference can, however, easily be misinterpreted because white couples are more likely to use contraceptive techniques, or to marry after the discovery of a premarital conception. Moreover, the illegitimacy rate among whites appears to be increasing, whereas that of nonwhites is, if anything, going down.

Still, Negroes are much less likely to belong to intact families than whites. This fact adds interest to the question of whether there is more alienation among the Negro population than the white.

Voluntary Associations

There is some evidence that membership in voluntary associations reduces an indivdual's sense of powerlessness and alienation. One survey [3] attempted to measure the extent to which a sample group felt they had control over the events that affected them. The responses, especially those of manual workers, suggested that members of a labor organization consistently had lower "powerlessness" scores than those who did not belong to any organization. The results are given in table 4.

TABLE 4.—*Mean scores on powerlessness for unorganized and organized manual workers, with income controlled (N=244)*

Income	Unorganized	Organized
Under $3,000	2.50 (14)	2.20 (5)
$3,000–4,999	3.20 (46)	2.81 (52)
$5,000–6,999	3.20 (25)	2.55 (75)
Over $7,000	3.00 (4)	2.65 (20)
Total (mean)	3.08 (89)	2.64 (153)
S.D.	1.5	1.8

NOTE.—Scores on the powerlessness scale ranged from 0 to 7.

[3] From A. Neal and M. Seeman, "Organizations and Powerlessness: A Test of the Mediation Hypothesis," *American Sociological Review* (1964), 29, 216–226.

Though the evidence is ambiguous, those with the most pronounced sense of powerlessness and alienation often seem to display an ambivalent attitude toward political participation. On the one hand, they are less likely to vote, keep track of political issues, and the like. On the other hand, there is also some evidence that they are disproportionately active in particular circumstances. Some studies have suggested, for example, that alienated and powerless voters are especially likely to be vigorous opponents of fluoridation and school bond issues.[4]

These results are consistent with a theory advanced by a number of sociologists: alienation usually leads to political apathy; yet alienated people become easily aroused in certain circumstances, such as when extremist and totalitarian forces are gaining strength. We need to continue seeking further evidence on this and other explanations.

The Neighborhood

The immediate neighborhood, though not so important as a social unit as it once was, still has some significance. The slum neighborhood is of particular interest, since it generally has less organization and social structure. Slums have disproportionate numbers of people who suffer from social pathologies, and slum communities lack the internal structure to deal with these problems.

In fact, social problems—from family disruption to suicide—cluster in the slum. This does not necessarily mean that the problems could disappear if there were no slums. It is logically possible that people with problems gravitate to the slum.

However, there is evidence that suggests that personal and social pathologies are contagious, and that slums *generate* many problems which they have no way of controlling.

If the probability of falling victim to a social pathology is greatly increased if one is brought up in a slum, then the slum is more than a private problem. It is a public and social problem. Private action cannot be expected to cure the social contagions of the slum environment any more than it can deal adequately with contagious diseases. They demand organized action, and organization is what many slums above all lack.

The lack of organization and social structure in the Negro slum therefore appears to be a major problem, and probably one that is related to the recent civil disorders. Cohesion or solidarity would be a great asset for it would give Negroes collective strength both in making external demands (e.g., on city government, or employers), and in enforcing internal constraints (e.g., against delinquency and crime). Its relative absence leaves the individual Negro particularly vulner-

---

[4] J. S. Coleman, *Community Conflict* (Glencoe, Ill.: Free Press, 1957); W. A. Eamson, "The Fluoridation Dialogue," *Public Opinion Quarterly*, 1961, 24, pp. 527–537; J. E. Horton and W. E. Thompson, "Powerlessness and Political Negativism," *American Journal of Sociology*, 1962, pp. 485–493.

able to the unrestrained predations of persons within his community or outside it. The examples of the solidarity of other ethnic groups, such as Jews and Chinese, indicate the tangible assets community solidarity provides: political power, aid to those in trouble, and lending arrangements for those establishing or expanding businesses.

Alienation

The net effect of an individual's participation can be partially revealed by surveys which seek to find out whether the individual feels he has control over his own destiny, an intelligible part to play in social life, and values he shares with others. According to such surveys the degree of alienation is substantially different for different groups.

Negroes are much more likely to feel powerless and alienated than whites. A comparison of white and Negro employed men in Los Angeles, for example, showed the following results:

	Negro Choices (percent) (N=312)	White Choices (percent) (N=390)
1. a. Becoming a success is a matter of hard work; luck has little or nothing to do with it	58	77
b. Getting a good job depends mainly on being in the right place at the right time	42	23
2. a. By studying the world situation, one can greatly improve his political effectiveness	58	70
b. Whether one likes it or not, chance plays an awfully large part in world events	42	30
3. a. Wars between countries seem inevitable despite the efforts of men to prevent them	69	66
b. Wars between countries can be avoided	31	34

Studies have also indicated that the difference in the sense of powerlessness between Negroes and whites is not explained solely by differences in education. When a sample of whites and Negroes were asked to react to the statement that "There is not much I can do about most of the important problems that we face today," the proportions responding affirmatively, at different educational levels, were as follows:

Negroes	Percent	Whites	Percent
Less than 12 years education	73	Less than 12 years education	57
12 years or more	60	12 years or more	34

Most other minorities also show a high degree of powerlessness, though the Jewish minority appears to be an exception.

Some surveys have suggested that Negroes in integrated areas, or with relatively integrated life styles, tend to feel less powerlessness than Negroes in highly segregated circumstances. The willingness to use violence, by contrast, appears to be greater among Negroes with a high degree of powerlessness, at least according to one survey of the Watts area of Los Angeles.

Among white Americans, alienation is apparently less likely to show up as a feeling of powerlessness and more likely to show up as a conviction that socially disapproved means must be used to attain objectives. Alienation in this sense is greatest among those with lower socioeconomic status. Those who are the most alienated, moreover, tend to have considerable prejudice against members of minority groups.

Alienation accordingly appears to play a role both in the discontents of the black minority, especially those who feel violent means are necessary, and also among those in the white population who show most prejudice against minority groups. Its importance among disaffected young people is not in dispute.

Conclusion

A sense of community, which would do a great deal to lessen alienation, is only one of our social and political objectives. We also cherish individual freedom and equality which too much cohesion in our social groups can sometimes restrict. Some alienation may also be related to intellectual and artistic creativity, and thus socially desirable. Moreover, it often strengthens the forces of reform, and enables the society to change with the times.

Thus a sense of community is not the only good. But, as the present divisions in our society reveal, it is very much worth asking whether we have as much as we need.

Appendix

HOW CAN WE DO BETTER SOCIAL REPORTING IN THE FUTURE?

GOOD DECISIONS must be based on a careful evaluation of the facts. This truism is so often the basis for our most mundane behavior that we are seldom aware of its far-reaching significance. Most people do not decide whether to carry an umbrella without first checking the weather forecast or at least glancing out the window to see if it is raining. Yet, those policymakers and citizens who are concerned about the condition of American society often lack the information they need in order to decide what, if anything, should be done about the state of our society. Without the right kind of facts, they are not able to discern emerging problems, or to make informed decisions about national priorities. Nor are they able to choose confidently between alternative solutions to these problems or decide how much money should be allocated to any given program.

Deficiencies of Existing Statistics

Only a small fraction of the existing statistics tell us anything about social conditions, and those that do often point in different directions. Sometimes they do not add up to any meaningful conclusion and thus are not very useful to either the policymaker or the concerned citizen. The Government normally does not publish statistics on whether or not children are learning more than they used to, or on whether social mobility is increasing or decreasing. It does publish statistics on life expectancy and the incidence of disability due to ill health, but some diseases are becoming more common and others less common, and no summary measure indicating whether we could expect more healthy life has been available.

This lack of data would not be surprising if it were simply a result of a lack of interest in statistics, or support for statistical collection, in the Government. But at the same time that some bemoan the lack of useful statistics, others are concerned about the supply of government statistics outrunning our capacity to make use of them. One Congressman recently argued that "we may be producing more statistics than we can digest," and argued that the Federal output of statistics may soon leave us "inundated in a sea of paper and ink." A detailed report by a Congressional Committee concluded that in 1967 more than 5,000 forms were approved by the Bureau of the Budget, which were estimated to take almost 110 million man-hours to complete. According to the same study, at the end of 1967 the Federal Government employed 18,902 Federal statistical workers, and spent $88 million on automatic data processing, computer equipment, and statistical studies under contract with private firms.[1] Comments and studies such as these do illustrate the fact that some are concerned about a plethora of statistics at the same time that the lack of particular types of statistical information stands in the way of better policy choices. This paradox suggests that the needed statistics cannot in practice be obtained simply through a general expansion of statistical efforts, but rather require new ideas about what statistics ought to be collected.

The problem does not appear to be unnecessary duplication of statistical efforts, or thoughtless decisions about what statistics should be collected. The Office of Statistical Standards of the Bureau of the Budget guards against any duplication in statistical collection, strives for comparability of different statistical series, and generally coordinates the Federal statistical effort. The Bureau of the Census and other agencies that collect statistics also seek the best advice, both inside and outside the Government, on what statistics ought to be collected. Thus the problem cannot be ascribed to poor management or foolish decisions—it evidently has deeper roots.

One of these roots is the fact that many of our statistics on social problems are merely a by-product of the informational requirements of routine management. This by-product process does not usually produce the information that we most need for policy or scholarly purposes, and it means that our supply of statistics has an accidental and imbalanced character.

Another source of the shortcomings of our statistical system is the *ad hoc* character of the decisions about what statistics should be collected. Numerous and gifted as those who advise us about what statistics we need may be, they cannot be expected to develop a system of data collection which maximizes the value and coverage of the statistics obtained with respect to the cost and number of the statistics gathered. A series of more or less independent decisions, however intelligent, may not provide the most coherent and useful system of statistics.

---

[1] Subcommittee on Census and Statistics, Committee on Post Office and Civil Service, House of Representatives, *1967 Report of Statistical Activities of the Federal Government*, House Report 1071.

Social Indicators

A social indicator, as the term is used here, may be defined to be a statistic of direct normative interest which facilitates concise, comprehensive and balanced judgments about the condition of major aspects of a society. It is in all cases a direct measure of welfare and is subject to the interpretation that, if it changes in the "right" direction, while other things remain equal, things have gotten better, or people are "better off." Thus statistics on the number of doctors or policemen could not be social indicators, whereas figures on health or crime rates could be.

A large part of our existing social statistics are thus immediately excluded from the category of social indicators, since they are records of public expenditures on social programs or the quantity of inputs of one kind or another used for socioeconomic purposes. It is not possible to say whether or not things have improved when Government expenditures on a social program, or the quantity of some particular input used, increase.

The phrase "social indicators" evidently emerged in imitation of the title of the publication called *Economic Indicators*, a concise compendium of economic statistics issued by the Council of Economic Advisers.

The National Income statistics are, in fact, one kind of social indicator; they indicate the amount of goods and services at our disposal. But they tell us little about the learning of our children, the quality of our culture, the pollution of the environment, or the toll of illness. Thus other social indicators are needed to supplement the National Income figures. However, the National Income statistics provide a useful model which can help guide the development of other social statistics.

One of the chief virtues of the National Income statistics is their extraordinary aggregativeness. Over any significant period of time, the output of some of the goods produced in a country increases while the output of other goods decreases. In a depression the output of glass jars for home preserves may increase; during a period of rapid growth the consumption of cheaper goods may decline as people switch to substitutes of higher quality. Changing technologies and fashions also insure that the tens of thousands of different types of goods produced in a modern economy do not show the same patterns of growth or decline. The achievement of the National Income and Product Accounts is that they summarize this incredible diversity of developments into a single, meaningful number indicating how much an economy has grown or declined over a period. They summarize this awesome variety of experience so well that we can usually spot even the minirecession, and allow the testing of meaningful hypotheses about the relationship between the National Income, or its major components, and other aggregative variables, such as consumption or investment. Changes in the Nation's health, or in the danger of crime, are in some sense narrower and simpler than changes in the whole economy, yet they have not heretofore been successfully aggregated.

The aggregation involved in the construction of the National Income and Product Accounts is so successful in part because relative prices are used to determine the relative weight or importance to be given to a unit of one kind of output as against a unit of a different type of output. If the number of automobiles produced has gone up by half a million since last year, while the output of potatoes has fallen by half a million bushels, we need to know the relative importance of these two developments before we can begin to make a judgment about the movement of the economy as a whole. It would obviously be arbitrary to determine the relative importance of these two developments by comparing the weight in pounds of an average automobile and a bushel of potatoes. Thus the relative prices of automobiles and potatoes are used to weigh the relative importance of two such developments in the National Income and Product Accounts.

Relative prices at any given moment of time provide weights that are presumably meaningful in welfare or normative terms. This is because a consumer who rationally seeks to maximize the satisfaction he gets from his expenditures, in terms of his own tastes or values, will allocate his expenditures among alternative goods in such a way that he gets the same amount of satisfaction from the last dollar spent on each type of good. If he obtained more benefit from the last dollar spent on apples than from the last dollar spent on oranges, he would obviously be better off if he spent more on apples and less on oranges.

The almost universal reliance on such aggregative measures of a society's income should not, however, obscure the dangers of failing to look behind the aggregates. Imagine these two cases: in one case, the National Income remains constant over a year, and all of the industries have the same level of output over the year; in the other case, the National Income also remains constant, but about half of the industries grow and the other half decline. Obviously, the first economy would be stagnant, whereas the second would be undergoing significant change, including presumably shifts of resources from some industries to others. We would not see the profound differences in these two hypothetical situations simply by looking at the aggregate figures for the National Income: we also have to disaggregate.

But disaggregation is not the enemy of aggregation. Indeed, a consciously constructed aggregate is usually easier to break down into its components than most other statistics. A well-constructed aggregative statistic, like the National Income, can (in principle at least) be compared to a pyramid. At the base are the individual firms, sites of production, and individual income recipients. Just above are the industries and communities, and above them are the major sectors and regions. When the same goods are processed by several firms, double counting is avoided by counting only the "value added." At the top there is the National Income. Such a pyramid can usually exist only when there has been the consistent definition and procedure that aggregation requires, and this systematic approach probably facilitates disaggregation as well as aggregation.

The relevant point that emerges from an examination of the National Income and Product Accounts is that aggregation can be extraordinarily useful, and is compatible with the use of the same data in disaggregated form. The trouble is that the "weights" needed for aggregative indexes of other social statistics are not available, except within particular and limited areas. It would be utopian even to strive for a Gross Social Product, or National Socioeconomic Welfare, figure which aggregated all relevant social and economic variables. There are no objective weights, equivalent to prices, that we can use to compare the importance of an improvement in health with an increase in social mobility. We could in principle have a sample survey of the population, and ask the respondents how important they thought an additional unit of health was in comparison with a marginal unit of social mobility. But the relevant units would be difficult even to define, and the respondents would have no experience in dealing with them, so the results would probably be unreliable. Thus the goal of a grand and cosmic measure of all forms or aspects of welfare must be dismissed as impractical, for the present at any rate.

Examples of Social Indicators

Within particular and limited areas, on the other hand, some modest degree of aggregation is now possible. And even over a limited area, such aggregation can be extremely useful. Some of the possibilities for useful aggregation over a limited span are illustrated in the chapters of this report.

One aggregative index is the expectancy of *healthy* life (strictly, life expectancy free of bed-disability and institutionalization). This index weights each disease or source of disability in proportion to its effect in reducing length of life or in keeping a person in bed or institutionalized. If there is either a reduction in bed-disability due to a reduction in disease, or an increase in life expectancy when bed-disability is unchanged, the index will increase, as it should. Admittedly, this aggregative index is, like the National Income statistics, imperfect in some respects.[2] Yet, its degree of aggregation makes it much easier to do

---

[2] It does not deal with the disability which does not force people to bed. Though it weighs the serious disease more heavily than the lesser disease, since the serious disease more often results in death or in longer bed-disability than the minor disease, it makes no allowance for the difference in pain and discomfort per day among various diseases. Finally, it ranks death and permanent bed disability equally, which may not be in accord with our values.

systematic work at a general level on the relationship between health and life and various causal variables, such as medical inputs, income levels, and the like.

Another area in which limited aggregation is possible is that of crime. To determine how much the danger of being victimized by a criminal changes over time, we should weight each type of crime by the extent of harm suffered by the victim. The dollar values lost would provide good weights for larcenies and burglaries, but the loss from personal injury or death would have to be estimated or assumed.

Where changes in the extent of "criminality" (or conversely, "law-abidingness") in a population are at issue, different weights are needed. Though it presumably does not matter to the victim whether he is killed by manslaughter or murder, society puts a very different assessment on the two acts. Weights for an index of criminality can be obtained from surveys, which show that respondents of different classes and occupations tend to agree on the relative heinousness of different significant crimes. The results of the best known of these surveys are highly correlated ($r=.97$) with data on the average length of prison sentences for the same crimes.

Some aggregates do not require the cumulation of qualitatively quite different things. For example, in the Opportunity chapter the operative assumption is that social mobility along some one dimension tends to vary in proportion to social mobility along other dimensions. Thus the correlation coefficient indicating the association between the socioeconomic status of men working now, as measured by the social rank of their usual occupation, and the socioeconomic status of their fathers, measured in the same way, is an aggregative index of social mobility. Its aggregative character derives, not only from the geographic span of the sample, but also from the assumption that changes in occupational status are *representative* of the diverse and manifold changes entailed in any significant intergenerational change in socioeconomic status. The implicit aggregation entailed in using a representative variable is in principle inferior to the more explicit sorts of aggregation discussed earlier, but it is usually easier in practice, and probably more congenial to those who are not familiar with aggregative theories or data constructs.

The Next Step: The Development of Policy Accounts

Although the potential usefulness of several social indicators has been illustrated in this report, this work represents only a beginning. Hopefully, there will be continued studies of social indicators and their method of construction. At the same time we also need to encourage the collection of new and more socially relevant data. If a balanced, organized, and concise set of measures of the condition of our society were available, we should have the information needed to identify emerging problems and to make knowledgeable decisions about national priorities.

The next step in any logical process of policy formation is to choose the most efficient program for dealing with the conditions that have been exposed. Then there must be a decision about how much should be spent on the program to deal with the difficulty. If these two decisions are to be made intelligently, the society needs information on the benefits and costs of alternative programs at alternative levels of funding.

It might seem at first glance that the benefits of an operating program could be obtained directly from the social indicators, which would measure any changes in the relevant social condition and therefore in the output of a program. In fact, it is much more difficult to obtain information on the output of even an existing program than to obtain a social indicator. The condition of an aspect of a nation depends, not only on a particular public program, but also on many other things. Health and life expectancy, for example, depend not only on public health programs, but also on private medical expenditures, the standard of living, the quality of nutrition, the exposure to contagious diseases, and the like. Thus to determine the output of a public program we normally have to solve something like what the econometrician would call the "specification problem"; we have to identify or distinguish those changes in the social indicator due to the changed levels of expenditure on the public program. This is often not a tractable task, but it could contribute much to truly rational decision making.

The fact that rational policy necessitates linking social indicators to program inputs means that social indicators alone do not provide all of the quantitative information needed for effective decision making. Ultimately, we must integrate our social indicators into policy accounts which would allow us to estimate the changes in a social indicator that could be expected to result from alternative levels of expenditure on relevant public programs.

Though an impressive set of social indicators could be developed at modest cost in the near-term future, a complete set of policy accounts is a utopian goal at present. This does not mean that work on a more integrative set of statistics should be postponed. These accounts will never be available unless we start thinking about the statistics we need for rational decision making now, even if this only entails marginal changes in the statistics we already have. The social statistics that we need will almost never be obtained as a by-product of accounting or administrative routine, or as a result of a series of *ad hoc* decisions, however intelligent each of these decisions might be. Only a systematic approach based on the informational requirements of public policy will do.

Selected Ann Arbor Paperbacks
Works of enduring merit

AA 11 **LITERATURE AND PSYCHOLOGY** F. L. Lucas
AA 44 **ANTHROPOLOGY** Sir Edward B. Tylor
AA 45 **EDUCATION** Immanuel Kant
AA 47 **THE IMAGE** Kenneth E. Boulding
AA 48 **FRUSTRATION** Norman R. F. Maier
AA 52 **AUGUSTE COMTE AND POSITIVISM** John Stuart Mill
AA 53 **VOICES OF THE INDUSTRIAL REVOLUTION** John Bowditch and Clement Ramsland, ed.
AA 60 **THE STUDY OF SOCIOLOGY** Herbert Spencer
AA 65 **A PREFACE TO POLITICS** Walter Lippmann
AA 84 **YOUTHFUL OFFENDERS AT HIGHFIELDS** H. Ashley Weeks
AA 92 **RELIGION AND THE STATE UNIVERSITY** Erich A. Walter, ed.
AA 93 **THE BIRTH OF THE GODS** Guy E. Swanson
AA 98 **MONTESQUIEU AND ROUSSEAU** Emile Durkheim
AA 105 **FREE SOCIETY AND MORAL CRISIS** Robert Cooley Angell
AA 107 **THE INDIANS OF THE WESTERN GREAT LAKES, 1615-1760** W. Vernon Kinietz
AA 109 **MOUNTAIN WOLF WOMAN** Nancy Oestreich Lurie, ed.
AA 127 **ORGANIZED CRIME IN AMERICA: A Book of Readings** Gus Tyler
AA 148 **THE DROPOUT: Causes and Cures** Lucius F. Cervantes
AA 165 **PRISONER'S DILEMMA** Anatol Rapoport and Albert M. Chammah
AA 169 **THE VIEW FROM THE BARRIO** Lisa Redfield Peattie
AA 171 **TOWARD A SOCIAL REPORT** Department of Health, Education, and Welfare, with an Introductory Commentary by Wilbur J. Cohen

For a complete list of Ann Arbor Paperback titles write:
THE UNIVERSITY OF MICHIGAN PRESS ANN ARBOR